Praise for *Talking Story*

"Many dismiss traditional healing as being unscientific or superstitious, while others overly romanticize these healing modalities dismissing much that modern medicine has to offer. The value of Marie-Rose Phan-Lê's perspective is that her feet are planted in both the modern and traditional worldviews. *Talking Story* is a wonderful bridge that spans across many cultures presenting an expanded view of healing and wellbeing."

—PHIL BORGES, documentary photographer/filmmaker of *Enduring Spirit, Tibet: Culture On The Edge* and *CRAZYWISE*

"Marie-Rose Phan-Lê is a gifted writer and storyteller with inimitable style. In *Talking Story* she brings to life ancient cultures, traditional wisdom, and the healing arts solely to bring awareness in the hearts of all. She shows that beyond the threshold of analytical sciences is a world waiting to be explored and experienced, that we can immensely benefit from. I am sure this book will enrich many a soul seeking truth beyond the veil."

—BABA SHUDDHAANANDAA BRAHMACHARI, author of *Making Your Mind Your Best*

"This beautifully written, magical book is an engaging, honest, and often funny recounting of the author's epic journey to document spiritual healing traditions that are in danger of dying out of memory. The story is also an intimate one as author Marie-Rose reluctantly chooses to face her own fears and thus discovers the heart of what it truly means to be a healer, then and now."

—ROBIN ROSE BENNETT, herbalist, author of *The Gift of Healing Herbs* and *Healing Magic: A Green Witch Guidebook to Conscious Living*

D0029160

Talking Story

One Woman's Quest to Preserve
Ancient Spiritual and Healing Traditions

MARIE-ROSE PHAN-LÊ

North Atlantic Books
Berkeley, California

From *Rumi Daylight: A Daybook of Spiritual Guidance,* translated by Camille and Kabir Helminski. Copyright © 1994 by Camille and Kabir Helminski. Reprinted by arrangement with The Permissions Company, Inc., on behalf of Shambhala Publications Inc., Boston, MA. www.shambhala.com.

Published by

North Atlantic Books   Cover and book design by Suzanne Albertson with cover
P.O. Box 1237   design contribution by Jaylene Carrillo, Tim Carrillo,
Berkeley, California 94712   Scott Slack, and High Impact Inc.

All cover photos by © Thomas L. Kelly, www.thomaslkellyphotos.com except "Hands" photo by © Cora E. Edmonds, www.artxchange.org/art/cora-edmonds

Printed in the United States of America

Maps designed by: Jaylene Carrillo, Tim Carrillo, and High Impact, Inc.

The author has changed some names and omitted some places or recognizable details to protect the privacy of some friends, family members, and acquaintances mentioned in the book. Otherwise all other elements are based on actual events recalled to the best of the author's ability, recorded on videos, and written in journal entries.

Talking Story: One Woman's Quest to Preserve Ancient Spiritual and Healing Traditions is sponsored and published by the Society for the Study of Native Arts and Sciences (dba North Atlantic Books), an educational nonprofit based in Berkeley, California, that collaborates with partners to develop cross-cultural perspectives, nurture holistic views of art, science, the humanities, and healing, and seed personal and global transformation by publishing work on the relationship of body, spirit, and nature.

North Atlantic Books' publications are available through most bookstores. For further information, visit our website at www.northatlanticbooks.com or call 800-733-3000.

Library of Congress Cataloging-in-Publication Data

Phan-Lê, Marie-Rose.
Talking story : one woman's quest to preserve ancient spiritual and healing traditions / Marie-Rose Phan-Lê.
       pages cm
    Includes bibliographical references and index.
    Summary: "Documents the author's journey through the world of healing, from Hawaii to the Himalayas"—Provided by publisher.
    ISBN 978-1-58394-828-6 (alk. paper)
1. Phan-Lê, Marie-Rose. 2. Spiritual biography. 3. Travel—Religious aspects.
4. Healing—Religious aspects. 5. Storytelling—Religious aspects. I. Title.
    BL73.P49A3 2014
    203'.1092—dc23
    [B]   2014010427

1 2 3 4 5 6 7 8 9 UNITED 19 18 17 16 15 14

Printed on recycled paper

To all the healers and teachers who took the time to talk story with me, and in loving memory of those who have now passed on. May their stories live on in your hearts.

CONTENTS

Talking Story

In Hawaii, when an invitation is extended, the host or hostess will say, "Come over and let's talk story." Talking story is about taking the time to linger over the details of the mundane, to ponder the realms of the profound, and to surrender any structure of time or agenda. It is practicing the art of listening and of being present.

As I began production of the *Talking Story* documentary project, traveling from Hawaii to the Himalayas, it wasn't long before I realized that in order for me to access healing traditions and healers in remote areas of the world, I would have to practice talking story. There would be no hit-and-run interviews, no rigid film production schedules, no way to remain an anonymous gleaner of other people's wisdom and experiences. Talking story is about intimate connection—in order to earn the honor of hearing the stories of another, I had to be willing to reveal my own.

This posed quite a challenge for me, considering my background. I was born in Vietnam and spent some time in France before coming to the United States as a child. As with all well-assimilated immigrants, I was taught that survival depended on my ability to blend in. It's no wonder that the myth of the objective "documentarian," a scientist of sorts separated from her subjects by a veil of romance or a lens of scrutiny, was so appealing to me.

My plan to remain unseen didn't last long, for with most healers or spiritual leaders I wished to meet, I first had to walk the gauntlet of the gatekeepers, a series of bridge people who could lead me to the inner sanctum of the healers. Imagine my dismay at realizing that in order to advance in my quest, I would have to reveal who I was, where my family came from, what I was seeking, what I intended to do with the gift of their knowledge, and what I needed to heal within myself. If I made it past the gatekeepers and was judged to be of pure heart and intention, my team and I would be permitted to proceed with the work and I would be allowed to state my case to the master healers.

The more I was willing to shed my self-consciousness, my fear of being exposed, or my presentation of who I thought I should be, the more I learned from the people I got to know. As much as I wanted to be open, however, I truly did not wish to speak of my own healing heritage. And yet this was the one thing that, in the end, opened greater doors to deeper dialogue. I did not want to reveal that my great-grandfather was a blind man who could see the past and the future, and my aunt channeled deities to heal people, nor that this aunt had told me I had the gift of healing and was being tested. My mother funneled her healing abilities in a perfectly acceptable form: she became a registered nurse, and my brother, following in her footsteps, became an anesthesiologist. I had greater confidence in my filmmaking abilities than in my healing abilities. Rather than becoming a healer, I decided I would best serve the greater good by making a documentary about healing and spiritual traditions.

I found myself the reluctant heroine, not in comic-book terms of having excess courage or superpowers, but in terms of being propelled into the everyman's or everywoman's path toward exploration and discovery as outlined by mythologist Joseph Campbell. It is only now that I understand I was the unwitting protagonist swept up by an archetypal heroic journey in which fate cast and directed her. In looking back, every step that was presented to me could not have fallen more perfectly in place had it been scripted by a Hollywood writer—from hearing the call to adventure, crossing the threshold from the ordinary into the extraordinary world, meeting mentors, facing tests and trials, seizing the sword, and returning with the elixir. I did it not with full abandon but always holding on to doubt and questioning what I was doing. I wanted to make this story about the healers, the fading traditions, the making of a documentary film—anything but about myself.

Yet, if I was not sure of what I was doing, I was at least willing to go along for the ride. I practiced talking story, and in doing so, I was able to have a deeper understanding of what it means to be a shaman, medium, doctor, teacher, and healer and what it means to heal. I learned about reciprocity—for everything I wished to receive, I had to be willing to make an offering. I learned my job was not so much about preservation—capturing something as it is and keeping it in stasis—but more about regeneration—turning loss into life, death into renewal. I learned that medicine from one culture, no matter how foreign, could benefit people of another culture if its use could be recontextualized with meaning to those who would receive the remedy. I learned that indeed we are in danger of losing large chapters of our collective physical and spiritual pharmacopoeia, but that it is possible to transform ancient practices into applications for the modern world. And I learned that like talking story, unlike storytelling where there is a clear beginning, middle, and end, the path to the finish is not clearly defined, for there is still opportunity to discover, to recover, and to change the foreseeable outcome.

My friend Pablo Amaringo, a retired Amazonian shaman, said as we walked through an area of the rain forest that was destroyed by logging, "Cutting down a tree is like burning a book before it has been read." Although we may not be able to stop the fires, my hope is that we at least open the book, become aware of what we are at risk of losing, and perhaps find a way to generate something new with the seeds of what remains.

PROLOGUE

Event Horizon

I don't like to think about it. Whenever I do, the same feelings overtake me—nausea, repulsion, and an unshakeable urge to leave the scene. I squirm and can't remain seated. I am forced to think about it now because I am interviewing editors for my documentary film on indigenous healers and mystics—a work in progress for nearly a decade. Viewing the video-tapes is like watching a dream that is so strongly with me, yet whose details and meaning escape me.

"Why don't you show us your most interesting footage?" suggests Nazeli, my post-production producer, who has arranged a meeting with some potential editors at her editing facilities. With over seventy hours of footage, finding the most compelling footage might seem a difficult choice, but it's not. The challenge, rather, has to do with whether or not I'm ready to go through this again. I know the most intriguing images are the hardest for me to face—and even this many years later, it doesn't seem to get any easier. But I can't stall any longer, for everyone gathered here is eagerly anticipating the viewing of the crown jewels—the centerpiece of our would-be masterpiece.

I try to give some context for what they're about to see by leading in with, "Something happened to me in the Himalayas of Nepal, and we caught it on camera. I don't remember a lot of it." Blake, the editing assis-tant, puts in the first tape, and I ask him to keep the volume low. As it cues up, my breathing becomes shallow and my mouth feels dry. I feel my pulse accelerating in my neck. I take a drink of cold water and remind myself that I'm here, in an editing suite at Sunset Edit in Hollywood, California. At first, it's the uncontrollable sobbing that I find so disconcerting, then the unintelligible words, followed by wailing, especially when the images reveal that noise is coming from me. We see me in trekking clothes, on the ground at the house of a *dhami* (shaman), struggling to communicate.

I exhale, forcing myself to breathe as I once again witness the footage I know all too well: on screen, the villagers scramble all around me while two of my crewmembers are at my side looking extremely worried. The shaman, Dhami Mangale, pats my forearm and says something that has the tone of, "There, there ... it's okay." His assistant, Tsering, gives me a metal cup full of sacred water, which I later find out had been painstakingly collected from a holy lake in Tibet the previous summer. I cringe now as I watch images of myself drinking it greedily and splashing it all over my face. The reel ends with my being carried down a wooden ladder on the back of Rinchinpo, one of our trek guides, who is dwarfed by my limp body. As distraught as witnessing this again makes me feel, my ego is intact enough to make a mental note for the future edit: exclude this shot—my butt looks gigantic, and the socks with butterflies on them, not a very cool look for a trekker chick. Then we see Thomas, our translator and co-producer, move quickly past the lens of the camera, looking concerned as he says, "She was speaking a language none of us understood."

Blake changes tapes and it's a good time for me to excuse myself. The nausea feels as intense as it did that day. My legs feel wobbly as I head down the stairs. I don't remember the details we just witnessed, but the feelings and physical sensations are palpable, as if this were happening again today. In the women's restroom, I use the same technique we use at high altitudes to prevent hyperventilation—exhale, exhale, inhale, exhale, exhale, inhale. I splash my face with water and in an instant I am taken back to the memory of that cup of sacred water from Lake Manasarovar in Tibet—how it cooled my skin and trickled down my throat quenching a thirst I hadn't known existed. It helped to calm me then. Now I look in the mirror and collect myself.

When I return to the editing suite, I see that they've rolled on without me. I enter quietly and am confronted with images of myself writhing on the floor and being lashed with a yak-hair whip by the dhami as he shouts, "Hey! Ho! Hey!" He blows onto seeds he holds in his closed fist and throws them against my body. Even then I knew he was performing an exorcism. It looks like it should have hurt, but I remember only that it hurt my feelings to be treated like some kind of unwelcome demon. Everyone viewing the footage is mesmerized, yet I feel embarrassed and find myself fighting the urge to explain away my bizarre behaviors as simply an intense case of altitude sickness. I have to leave again. It's fear that sends me away this time. It's mounting as it always does when I know we're getting close to this part. I know what comes next, but only because I've watched the tapes so often. If we didn't have this evidence, I'm not sure I'd have chosen to remember any of this. But there were witnesses, of course—my crew, the villagers, and the shaman. Still, there's an undeniable power the physical images hold. What's about to unfold on the video screen is a long struggle that would last close to eight hours—a struggle to come back to my body while something—some external force—was keeping me away. Away from my frantic film and trek crew, away from the desperate attempts of the dhami to extract the interloper, away from my own body, away from this reality. What I do remember clearly is feeling terrified that I might never return.

I muster up the courage to head back into the editing room. When I enter, everyone looks at me expectantly. I know I won't be able to explain what they just saw, but I can tell how it came to be.

CHAPTER 1

Connectivity

Seattle (the Ordinary World)

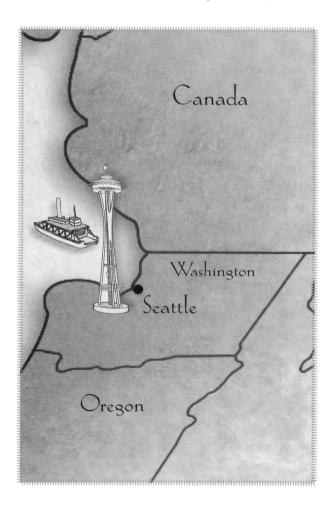

I put the *mala* beads to my nose and inhale the sweet scent of sandalwood. As I put them around my neck, I think of the Tibetan Buddhist monk who'd taken them off his own neck and given them to me. In so doing, he'd passed along to me all the mantras and intentions of compassion he'd infused into them. It has been nearly a decade, and the cords of the tassels are frayed and the brightness of their gold and red faded, but the power of protection that emanates from them is never diminished. I say my prayer: "Mother, Father, Spirit, God, allow me to be of greatest service to the one before me. Allow her to receive the strength, courage, and healing she needs to stay on her path of highest good. Allow any energy that is appropriate to come through me to do so at this time. Allow anything that no longer serves her to be released. Thank you for allowing me to do this work."

Suddenly that old familiar feeling comes over me. My heart feels like it's going to explode and I am filled with a sense of well-being—like the passion of falling in love. I shift from seeing the furnishings and walls around me to seeing into another place and time. My hands begin to shake and I place them on my patient's head. I feel myself pulling out mental constructs that no longer serve her: "I'm not good enough," "I'm not supported," "I can't be who I really want to be." I lay my hands on her heart and tears begin to seep through her closed lids. I see so many disappointments. I move my hands to her lower abdomen and see invaders—those who did not hold this space as sacred. I cut the cords between her and them. Lighting the stick of *palo santo,* a sacred wood from Peru, I blow a cleansing breath into the top of her head, filling her with light and love. I run the wooden mallet around the lip of a Tibetan singing bowl; it evokes the tones of the heart as it vibrates. When she sits up from the healing table, she tells me, "I feel so full and yet so light."

I reply, "This is you without all the baggage. Remember this feeling." As we sit on the couch, I share what I saw while she was on the table, and she confirms a history of abuse, a string of heartbreaks, and multiple problems with her reproductive system. She adds that despite being successful in the corporate world, she never feels good enough, so she's driving herself, her marriage, and her soul into the ground. She wants to know another way of being. She is ready to learn and heal. And then she asks me, "How did you do it? How did you go from being in the film industry and working in high-tech to being a healer?"

Although it has been years since I accepted this as my calling, it's only now that I feel I can answer with clarity. "It was identity theft," I answer. "I had to lose my sense of who I was, or thought I was supposed to be, in order to connect with my authentic self."

It was the end of the twentieth century and there was an air of excitement—the anticipation of the arrival of the new millennium. Seattle was booming with the success of the technology industry and I worked for the top dog. I had been hired because this company was looking for people who could bridge between the entertainment industry and the world of new interactive media, and I had been working in film and television for over a decade by then. I was doing pretty well for myself, and for the first time in my life, my family could finally sort of understand what I was doing for a living, if only because the company I worked for was a household name. The promise of connectivity—creating community—through infotainment, Web portal sites, and interactive television was enticing.

By day, I perceived myself to be a fairly normal person going to work in an office—although it was pretty obvious I didn't quite fit in when I decorated my office with a Zen fountain and put crystals on my computer and a Buddha statue on the bookcase, or when I would show up to team meetings in thigh-high boots, taking full advantage of the lack of a formal dress code. Despite the corporate climate, this particular corporation prided itself on allowing freedom of expression and creativity to nurture genius and productivity. I took this as an opportunity to embrace both my spiritual side and my sassy attitude, figuring it would be acceptable, or at least tolerated, as long as I could perform. And perform I did. With my immigrant work ethic and type triple-A personality, I earned the freedom to make my own schedule and run my own projects.

By night, I studied healing and spirituality with my teacher, having been swept up by the spiritual growth of the New Age movement of the eighties and nineties. I had yearned for a teacher for years. As a child, I had some experiences that the adults around me could not explain. I recall seeing my father walking up the stairs of our home in Vietnam—after he had passed away. When I asked my nanny about it at the time, she chided me, "Don't tell anyone about this. People will call you crazy. They'll send you away." I believed her, and felt something that had been light become dark and heavy. Only now can I name it as shame for speaking something that should have been kept secret. I remember knowing what people were thinking and what they needed. And I was no angel. This knowledge allowed me to figure out how to get my way. As I got older, this knowing was always with me, but it felt more like a Muzak version of a song I couldn't get out of my head. Besides, since I attended French Catholic school from the age of three, both in Vietnam and France, I was too busy trying to look normal to avoid the inevitable beatings from the nuns, or later, from the American kids who taunted me with, "Chinese, Japanese, dirty knees—woo, look at these!" as they flipped my skirt up to reveal my underpants.

Then, in my late twenties, "The gift came back with a vengeance," as I'm fond of saying. I began to know things I shouldn't have been privy to because there were no logical explanations for how I'd come to know them—the details of a coworker's marital struggles, a fellow flight passenger's neck injury, a secret hand signal used only between my former husband and his deceased brother. At times my heart would feel like it might explode out of my chest if I didn't pass on to others the information I received for them, whether it was "You need to dump the guy," or "You need to see a doctor." And I must admit that my delivery in those early days was not very gracious.

I began to sense things that frightened me, like negativity in certain places or illness in people. These incidents felt overwhelming, and I felt

I needed some help in understanding what exactly was happening. Part of me questioned my sanity. I needed a teacher or guide. What I didn't want was to worship a guru, as I'd seen so many others do, but to obtain an apprenticeship. I wanted to be in the presence of someone who practiced spiritual healing and who could give me lessons in a lecture-and-lab format—something like the premed courses I took back in college. I wasn't consciously looking to become a healer; after all, I had given up that notion when I switched my major from medicine to media and marketing. But I longed to have a greater understanding of my peculiar experiences and to have a better grasp of the greater metaphysical realms.

I was led to my teacher because an acquaintance told me of a woman healer and spirit medium who was offering apprenticeships. She'd used the very term I had—apprenticeship—and I took it as a sign. I spent the last five years of the nineties under this teacher's tutelage, living as a member of her household, just as it might have been done in the old days of true apprenticeship. I attended channelings, healing sessions, and read everything I could get my hands on about ancient and New Age spirituality and healing. I left the big corporation and struck out on my own to freelance as a consultant to companies and organizations whose missions matched my ideals of bringing positive change into the world. I was beginning to feel my worlds becoming more integrated. I felt at once free and frightened at not knowing what might lie ahead.

In the fall of 1999, I returned from a vacation in France—a much-needed break from the stress of that summer. In the early months of summer, my teacher's health had taken a turn for the worse, and I was a member of her core support team. As her most devoted student, I had been entrusted to give her daily healing sessions. Through prayers, healing work, the support of our community, and caring allopathic and naturopathic doctors, she was able to avoid leg amputation. She did have to sacrifice a toe, however, as well as undergo triple bypass surgery for her ailing heart. She was to remain in the hospital while I was in France, and we'd both agreed that the timing for me to go couldn't have been better. I'd get some reprieve while she mended.

Leading up to her illness, however, I had begun to question her methodology and integrity. I finally took a break and went to France to get a fresh perspective. While I was away, I was able to come to terms with the fact that she was human, and that I'd matured from being her apprentice to being a friend or equal. In the process, however, I'd witnessed her "fall from grace." This seemed like something we could discuss openly, and I believed she would want an accountability partner. But I also pondered how much her undiagnosed or denied diabetes played a role in the demise of her spiritual foundation. All of it was weighing heavily on my mind that first night back as I began sorting through my piles of mail that had accumulated during my monthlong sojourn.

During my time in France, I'd reunited with the couple—*tonton* (uncle) and *tata* (aunty)—who'd "adopted" my siblings and me during my formative years while my mom was stranded in Vietnam. My visit with them helped to heal some old wounds around having been forced to leave my beloved tonton and tata at the age of six to join my mother and her new husband in the United States. They told tales of having to scramble to keep ahead of nosy neighbors, prying authorities, and speculation as to how this French couple ended up with four Vietnamese kids in Marseilles. I complained about the abusive nuns and priests who ran the schools my siblings and I had to attend, but Tata rebuked me, saying, "Hush up, child. Those people agreed to let you attend their schools, no questions asked." She advised me to forgive them.

To aid with my reluctance to give the nuns a break, I recruited my best friend and favorite travel companion, Giselle, to join me on a pilgrimage to Lourdes in the southwest of France. Here, an apparition of the Virgin Mary was said to have appeared to the now sainted Bernadette in the 1800s. I had visited Lourdes as a child and remembered being mesmerized by the grotto filled with hundreds of crutches left by those who no longer needed them as evidence of the miraculous healings that took place there.

Giselle and I waited in line for hours at the women's bathhouse to be plunged into the blessed waters, surrounded by a chorus of women from all over the world saying prayers in their respective languages on their rosaries. It was a mix of calming meditative prayer and rising anxiety as closing time approached and hundreds of women were still waiting their turn. Giselle and I somehow made it to the baths that day. We were given gowns to wear over our undergarments. The assisting nuns instructed me to kiss a plastic statue of the Virgin Mary, which had bright red lipstick residue on her from some previous worshipper. The nun plunged me backward into a big tub of extremely cold water fed from the sacred grotto. I was surprised to find that I actually felt a powerful rush of love and well-being coming over me, as if I'd been somehow sanctified by the essence of the divine feminine. Although these nuns were just as austere as any other nun I had ever known, they were clearly in service to a higher authority. I felt safe with them. I made a conscious choice at that moment to bring this compassion I'd been blessed with to my teacher, who had taught me so much about spiritual realms, and yet who was plagued with so much human frailty.

Among the stack of mail back home, I noticed several bills in my name from a variety of credit card companies with whom I was sure I'd never applied for any accounts. As I scanned the charges—huge amounts for purchases I never made—I instinctively started scanning the house, seeking an explanation. With every step I took down the stairs that led me from my side of the house to hers, a sick realization was beginning to sink in, deeper and deeper. I looked around the space and saw many of the very items that had been charged in my name. It dawned on me that I would not have been the one to sort through the mail had she not been in the hospital.

My survival skills kicked in and I cancelled all the accounts. I filed a formal report with the police department. Some companies would never forgive the debt, which ended up being in the tens of thousands—surreal for someone who until then prided herself on paying off her credit card bills every month. I would spend the next few years pleading my case and paying every spare cent to keep my credit in good stead, all the while holding out hope that my teacher would one day come clean, show up with the money she owed, and realize her error in judgment.

What happened the night I called my teacher in her hospital room to tell her what I'd discovered should have been a clue that this notion was mere fantasy. Incredibly, I felt badly for having to discuss this disturbing issue with her while she was still recuperating. Even more incredibly, she had no remorse and nonchalantly said, "I'm sorry you're so upset. I know you're just scared, but don't worry. I'll cover the debts and make the payments like I've been doing all along." All along? It hadn't occurred to me that this had been going on for months, even years. And I never saw the bills because I was never the one to sort the mail.

Her words and tone were meant to calm and assure me that all was well, normal even, but they had the opposite effect. I felt like a light had been taken from me, and in its place was a numbing dense despair. Within twenty-four hours, I packed my things and promptly moved out with the help of two girlfriends and the man I liked to refer to as my favorite ex-husband. I ran as if my hair were on fire, the flames burning all bridges between my teacher and me to ash. To add insult to injury, word got back to me that it was being said that I was possessed by a dark evil spirit, which explained my behavior—the good student who became the bad seed and turned against her teacher. In a bizarre way, it would have been much easier to believe that than to know I was simply a fool who got sucker-punched. Being possessed by something outside of myself would have at least explained how I'd been so dispossessed of my right mind to have allowed myself to be so blatantly taken. If I had ever been the least bit tempted to be a spiritual teacher or healer, that notion was quickly dissolved. How could I ever trust myself again to discern right from wrong, reality from fantasy? The loss of faith in my teacher led to a loss of faith in myself, in my sense of judgment, in my own integrity and in the validity of all I had learned from her.

They call this crime identity theft. Yes, it was someone usurping my sense of self and using my privileges without my consent. But it was deeper than that, since I had to pay for her actions with more than just money. I would come to dramatically label this event as "spiritual rape"—the worst sanctuary invasion. Entrusting a teacher, guide, or healer with the care and development of my spirit, the most sacred aspect of self, opened up the possibility for the greatest level of intimacy and also the deepest level of betrayal. This wounding, however, gave me a precise clarity that has never left me: The immensity of the privilege and the burden of responsibility of any caregiver, especially a spiritual one, is one of the most sacred of all covenants.

My mom used to say, "What is bad is good," a testament to her survival skills and ability to make lemonade out of lemons. I knew that in order to recover from this and to forgive myself for letting it happen, I would eventually have to find what was good in all of this bad, and one day restore my faith. After all, I had been able to transform a painful divorce into a loving friendship. Of course, that took a lot of work on both our parts. This healing would be a solo project, and it would be up to me to find the meaning behind it over time. In the meantime, I did the only thing I knew to do: I dove into my work. I took a consulting job that had me spending four days a week in Los Angeles, allowing for a change of scenery and leaving only three days a week for me to face the emotional and financial aftermath of this transgression. No matter how busy I kept myself, however, I couldn't shake the feeling of shame for having been so deluded as to believe I was on the spiritual path only to wind up in the hole. There are two choices when you find yourself there—curl up and die or start clawing your way out. Another piece of mom wisdom.

Being my mother's daughter, I discovered fairly quickly that this incident did not squelch my desire to keep seeking spiritual truth and healing wisdom, but rather it fueled my drive to find better teachers and authentic healers. Maybe because this longing had lived in me before I met my teacher, it was a part of me she could not take, and it gave me something to grab onto.

Leading up to the identity theft, I had been growing increasingly disgruntled by the spiritual materialism of the New Age, and my teacher's using my credit to fill her world with things certainly didn't help the matter. Admittedly, as spiritual as I liked to see myself, I too was firmly engaged in the material. I drove a red convertible (a car my friend Lama Tenzin, a Tibetan Buddhist monk, deemed "The Selfish Car" because there was barely room to fit two people); liked being fashionable; and enjoyed the nicer things in life—fine meals, travel, and spa treatments. The fulfillment of these desires seemed to carry over into my spiritual pursuits. Although I still believe a greater spiritual awareness grew out of the New Age movement, I noticed those of us hungry for the sacred seemed to have an insatiable appetite to consume it. We had to buy the right crystals, the latest books, tickets to the coolest workshops; we made appointments with popular healers and psychics as if scheduling a manicure or facial. All this made me yearn to reach for the ancient traditions as they were being practiced within the context of their own cultures.

I wasn't aware of it then, but now I see that I'd always been a cultural anthropologist, not by trade or academic training, but by the necessities of survival and assimilation. I had lived in three countries, made homes in the West, South, Northwest, Southwest, and Mid-Atlantic of the United States, and was born in a war-torn country with a long history of being settled, invaded, and colonized. Learning to live within many different cultures required that I have the skills to study the other and to thrive as an other. My passion to study the loss of a culture's spiritual legacy—its view of the cosmos, its knowledge of its place in the universe, and its connection to the unseen world—may have been due to my home country's history and blended influences of religion, philosophy, and cosmologies, or my own feelings of disconnection to my cultural roots. I was deeply moved by the work of anthropologist and ethnobotanist Wade Davis, whose writings eloquently capture the beauty and loss of so many indigenous cultures suffering ethnocide—the destruction of a culture. I fancied the idea of myself as an "ethnospiritualist," one who studies how members of different cultures use their spiritual resources to adapt to the day-to-day choices of surviving and living.

When I wasn't doing consulting work, I spent my time doing research. With the miracle of modern technology and the World Wide Web, I was able to connect easily with people who were working in the field—anthropologists, ethnobotanists, photographers, and journalists. These experts underscored what I'd been reading—that indeed, the healing plants, people, and places of the world were quickly disappearing due to globalization, habitat destruction, and cultural assimilation. While I had lost my faith on the spiritual front, I was still confident in my professional abilities. I began to make a plan to use my experience in film, television, and technology to preserve and present the vanishing spiritual and healing traditions of indigenous cultures worldwide.

Looking back, I see how fate put together the perfect concoction to heal what was ailing me. It enticed me to take a heroine's journey by giving me a calling with all the right ingredients for my particular constitution. This assignment appealed to my escapist tendencies and offered a promise of adventure and an opportunity to take a leave of absence from licking my wounds. It involved a mission to "save the world," which was no doubt much easier than saving myself. And it allowed me to indulge in my favorite addiction to serve the greater good—workaholism.

The mission: present an expanded paradigm for healing by traveling the world, making a documentary film, creating an archive, and establishing a portal website to connect healers—those in modern medicine and ancient healing traditions. This would be my public service. My private quest would be to learn what it means to know oneself as healer or spiritual teacher. I wanted to ask the people I'd meet, "How do you balance your earthly concerns with spiritual commitments?" "What are the spiritual laws that shape your lives?" "What do you love about your calling?" "What do you hate about it?" "How did you walk the path from calling to mastery?"

I accepted this assignment with gusto. It confirmed what I already knew. I didn't need to be a healer myself to be a change agent on the planet. I could simply use my worldly skills to bring healing and spiritual knowledge to others through media. I would dedicate myself to seeking out the healers and sages who still held the mystical as sacred, and who knew nothing about the mundane realm of credit cards.

CHAPTER 2

Location Scouting

Peru (Call to Adventure)

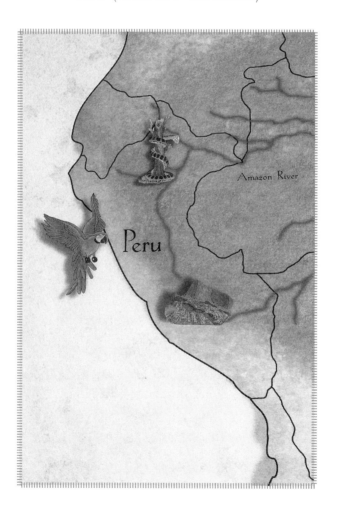

Suspended between earth and sky was my experience of life for many years after my teacher's betrayal, but especially in those first few months. As I was mired in the details of clearing my name and her monstrous debt, I was also reaching for the stars to realize my dream. In the spring of 2000, six months after I cut ties with my teacher, I found myself swaying on a rope and steel cable sky bridge, walking among the treetops of the rain forest canopy in Peru.

I felt uplifted among those giants that generously allowed me to traverse their limbs so I could, for a few moments, see a different perspective—and one that opened me up to the endless possibilities ahead. From that vantage point I had an unobstructed view of miles of verdant life in all directions. The canopy leaves made a blanket so dense that I could not see the ground that lay 120 feet below. What I did see when I dared to look down was a single orchid bloom whose stem extended from the side of a tree trunk. Orchids, despite their delicate appearance, are some of the hardiest plants on the planet—able to withstand heavy rains or long dry spells. This one was wise enough to position itself at just the right height, about one hundred feet above ground, to catch the perfect blend of sunlight, rain, and air circulation. I would later learn that the job of a good shaman is to be as the tree is to the orchid—a strong tether for the patient's or student's soul as it journeys to higher realms and a safe place for that soul to land and flourish when it returns home.

As I took in the viewpoint along the Canopy Walkway, I couldn't help but pinch myself at my luck. I'd just realized two things on my dream wish list: meeting my first Amazonian shaman, and exploring the rain forest canopy. And the frosting on the cake was that I was being paid as a media consultant to do a feasibility study, or "location scout," as it's known in the film industry. The client was a small California-based pharmaceutical company developing medicine from the *sangre de grado (Croton lechleri),* or dragon's blood tree—and its goal was to promote cultural exchange and build awareness about the medicinal value of rain forest plants in Peru. It was a mix of moxie and serendipity that had gotten me here.

While doing research in Seattle, I'd decided to let everyone know what I was up to, figuring that casting a wide net among friends and colleagues might allow me to snag some leads to fund my project. I sent emails, made phone calls, surfed the web, took meetings, and even did some old-fashioned research at the library. All this was part of my two-part strategy—action mixed with intention. In addition to what I was doing out in the world, in the privacy of my own condo I'd started a list on my corkboard, pinning corresponding images of places and cultures I wanted to visit: the Amazonian rain forest, Hawaii, Mongolia, Tibet, Nepal, Vietnam, India, and China to start. I looked at the board several times a day and added any symbols, words, or images that might help me draw this dream out of the ether and into reality.

With connectivity in play, I found the company that would provide my ticket to the Peruvian rain forest. It came through a connection to a colleague I'd met at the high-tech company I'd worked for. What appealed to me about this small California-based company, besides its very charismatic CEO, Lisa, and its knowledgeable ethnobotanists, physicians, and anthropologists, was its commitment to working with the indigenous communities. In addition to developing medicine from the dragon's blood tree in Peru, they also hoped to create a sustainable economic model that would benefit the local people while preserving the environment and making rain forest medicine more readily accessible. I was so enthusiastic about the company's mission, yet the first time I saw the images of a worker drawing resin from the dragon's blood tree, with its heart-shaped leaves, I was surprised by my emotional reaction. As diagonal slits were cut into the tree's trunk, a deep-red sap oozed from the wounds. As it bled, I wept.

My charge as a media consultant was to create a media platform to document and define the company's mission to potential investors. I also pitched the idea of an Internet-based children's cultural exchange pilot program for their nonprofit arm. I was immediately dispatched to Peru to be immersed in the company's work. Nothing could have been a greater answer to the call to adventure.

Any call to adventure, of course, requires preparation. My forte in film and video pre-production planning was something in which I had great confidence. Planning for my personal needs was a bit more tricky. Although I lived in the birthplace of REI (Recreational Equipment Inc.), a mecca for outdoor gearheads, I was challenged to find expedition wear that was, well, stylish. Let's face it, if you happen to be a curvy girl who is slight of stature, "sport casual" clothing can evoke a chunky SpongeBob SquarePants look. After much dressing-room trauma, I finally managed to find multipocketed quick-drying convertible zip-into-shorts trekking pants that didn't make my backside look like I was wearing diapers, along with lightweight moisture-wicking wrinkle-resistant sun-protective button-up shirts with hidden pockets that minimized my bustline. To complete my ensemble, I added what I already had: a North Face Gore-Tex shell, previously tested on film shoots that required withstanding hours under the Seattle rain, snowstorms of the Cascade Mountains, and the winds of the Columbia River Gorge, and my Doc Martens Goth boots, a necessary part of every Seattleites wardrobe in the late nineties. I was far from chic, but I was satisfied.

Besides gathering the necessary supplies, I also had to endure the slew of recommended travel vaccinations for Peru: hepatitis A, typhoid, yellow fever, hepatitis B, rabies, measles-mumps-rubella, and tetanus-diphtheria. My visit to the travel clinic was anything but reassuring. Although I believe that nurses and doctors generally mean well, their scare and shaming tactics, especially where travel abroad is concerned, tend to trigger the rebel in me. Because this opportunity to go to Peru came so quickly, I only had enough lead time to receive the hep A series, and I opted to omit the hep B. I had the mindset, however misguided, that I could pick à la carte from the recommended vaccination menu.

One nurse tried to dissuade me from going altogether until I could get the hep B series. Then, when I had refused the rabies series and the antimalarial drug and told her I would be visiting shamans who would know how to deal with these ailments, she raised her eyebrow and said, in the most condescending tone, "Do you realize how dirty, risky, and infectious this type of travel can be? You do understand you will be traveling in a Third World country?" I simply looked at her and replied, "I was born in a Third World country, okay? And look, I survived."

I knew it wasn't wise to argue with someone who was trying to help me to remain healthy, but I remembered all the vaccinations I'd gotten to enter the United States as a child, and I didn't relish getting more than I thought I needed. I did agree to fill a prescription of a prophylactic for malaria that is much better than its alternative, mefloquine, which can cause vomiting, dizziness, and depression. I could've handled that, but nightmares, psychosis, hallucinations, and seizures? Those side effects sounded worse than what malaria might do to me. In the end, I never took a single pill, although I wouldn't recommend rebellion over reason when it comes to tropical diseases. Perhaps as a reminder not to fight against those who are trying to help you, every side effect that a person could possibly get from vaccinations I suffered in spades—soreness surrounding the injection sites, extreme fatigue, severe headaches, fever, and muscle aches. And all this before I'd even packed my bags. And yet, I knew what lay ahead would make all the pain worthwhile.

Patience is the key to navigating Peru's jungles, waterways, and the politics of working with local gatekeepers and guides. In fact, it's the key to navigating any quest for something other than the familiar. I'd done my best to plan for the trip, even going so far as taking Spanish immersion classes, but nothing prepared me for the slamming on the brakes of my habitual go-go-go get-it-done attitude. I had only one week to cover a lot of ground, so I landed in Lima, Peru's capital, ready to make things happen. I would eventually learn that putting oneself in the position to allow things to happen is a lot more efficient and magical than making things happen. But at that time I had been trained and rewarded for being a go-getter, so I was determined to use sheer will to accomplish everything on my "to do" lists.

My time in Lima consisted of four hours of sleep, half an hour for breakfast, and a trip to the airport for a flight to Pucallpa, a city in eastern Peru that sits along the banks of the Ucayali River, a major tributary of the Amazon. Elsa, a Peruvian ethnobotanist, and our translator, Carina, a blond, blue-eyed beauty of Mexican-Swedish descent, were my welcoming committee. They would be my lovely companions for the rest of this adventure, accompanying me to the villages along the Ucayali River and to the rain forest canopy. Lisa, the CEO of the company I was working for, and her seven-year-old son, Bobby, who we later deemed the cultural exchange ambassador, joined us for the first few days of the journey.

At the airport, we got our first indication that delays would be the recurring theme for the trip when Elsa's backpack was stolen. She'd put it down to review our paperwork and in an instant it, and the thief who took it, had disappeared. Elsa was so upset and yet she kept apologizing to us. When I asked her why she was apologizing, reminding her that she was the victim of a crime, she said, "I don't care about my bag. I'm just so sad that this would be your first impression of my country and my people." As it turned out, it was Elsa, not the thief, who in that moment and in the days that followed left an indelible impression of the heart of the Peruvian people.

Pucallpa, "red earth" in the indigenous language of the region, was our base camp for the first three days. This meant it was basically the place where we would collapse each evening and breakfast each morning. The plans we'd enthusiastically make at breakfast, however, were never the actualities we'd experienced by day's end. Maybe it was being on an adventure full of new experiences that allowed me to begin to release my control-freak ways, or it could have been the *mate de coca* (tea made with the leaves of the coca plant—yes, the very same one cocaine is derived from) we drank daily that helped me feel at once relaxed and rejuvenated. Coca tea is known by the people of this part of South America as the messenger of the gods and is highly regarded for its medicinal benefits, such as combating fatigue and altitude sickness, calming digestive disorders, regulating blood sugar and carbohydrate metabolism, and elevating mood. Whatever it was, I felt a freedom and lightheartedness I hadn't experienced in a long time.

Our first day in Pucallpa pretty much exemplified the need-for-patience rule. We were supposed to go straight from the Pucallpa airport and travel by boat to a small community of indigenous Shipibo-Conibo villagers. When we arrived, the boat driver who was supposed to meet us at the airport and take us upriver was nowhere in sight. Arriving at our hotel by taxi, we found out the boat driver was still at the airport waiting for us. During the time that Elsa went back to the airport to meet him, he had come to meet us at the boat dock. As we walked along the riverbank through clusters of colorful shacks and rubbish piles to get to the port and meet the Shipibo-Conibo leader, we found out that he had gone to his father's inland home. By then, it was too late to make the hour and twenty-minute boat ride upriver. So, inland we went to find the community leader's father's home. When we arrived, we found out that father and son had gone to the airport looking for us. Ah ... to have had a cell phone then.

And, just like in any adventure movie, our series of mishaps ended with a good old-fashioned car-stuck-in-the-mud scene. We'd arrived at the end of rainy season in late April, so many of the local roads that had been underwater, traversable only by boat a few short weeks earlier, remained a terrain of very slippery clay. So, here we were: four women, a child, and a very stressed taxi driver pushing, pulling, and hypothesizing about the best way to get the car on the move again. As luck would have it, we found a fallen branch to put under one of the tires and gave it our all with a series of heave-hos while the taxi driver stepped on the gas. Once the car was freed, the driver mournfully tried to wipe the thick coat of mud off his car with his handkerchief. I felt awful when I later found out that for all his troubles, the driver's fare, though considered fair market rate, amounted to only ten U.S. dollars.

Amazingly enough, despite our fire-drill antics, we still got a lot accomplished with what remained of the day. Most encouragingly, I had the opportunity to meet my very first authentic Amazonian *curandero* (shaman). I had been used to seeing the urban neo-shamans of the New Age in Seattle adorned with jaguar teeth, feathers, rattles, and very serious fierce facades, so I wasn't sure what to expect when I met Pablo. I grew increasingly excited as we drove to the Usko Ayar Amazonian School of Painting, the art school he'd established for the underprivileged children in Pucallpa and its neighboring villages. My heart pounded as if I were a rabid fan about to meet her favorite rock star. We traveled along the pot-holed red mud roads, passing thatched roof homes along the way. Once we arrived, we walked across narrow wooden planks toward the school building, a brightly painted blue wooden structure built on stilts that was topped by the luxury of a tin roof. At the open doorway, I met Pablo Amaringo, a well-known curandero, who greeted me with a sweet smile and gentle eyes. He was dressed in country club casual—a denim button-up shirt and pressed khaki pants. As I got to know him, Pablo continued to surprise me with the unexpected.

Little Bobby, who didn't speak Spanish and had never been to Peru before, didn't hesitate to jump right into a painting lesson with the Peruvian kids. It was led by Wellington, an Usko Ayar alumnus. When Wellington first met Pablo, he was struggling with recurring malaria that he'd contracted during his military service. He often felt so debilitated by the symptoms, such as fevers, extreme fatigue, sweating, and nausea, that it was difficult for him to find regular work. Pablo not only treated his malaria with a tea made from the bark of a rain forest tree, but encouraged Wellington's interest in the arts by teaching him to draw and paint. Like the many other former students of Usko Ayar, Wellington, now in his twenties, makes a living as an artist and gives a percentage of each painting he sells back to the school. In this practice of reciprocity, he's paying forward what was given to him to support future students. There is no tuition for the school, so as a nonprofit organization, Usko Ayar, which means "spiritual prince" in the Quechua language, is supported by donations and its former students. Wellington explained that Pablo not only teaches art, but also about how to live with humbleness, sincerity, and respect for fellow beings, including the rain forest plant spirits and Pachamama (Mother Earth). Extending Usko Ayar's reach, Wellington had spent a year teaching and living in a Shipibo village upriver. The villagers named him "Wonder Hands" because of the beautiful jaguar paintings those hands could create.

While Lisa proudly watched her son learning to paint jaguars and rain forest life, and Elsa and Carina spoke to the other teachers and students, I had the opportunity to speak with Pablo alone. This was a privilege and I was thrilled. I followed him to a small office in the schoolhouse. Once I set up the video camera and had my pen and paper ready to record Pablo's pearls of wisdom, it dawned on me that there was no translator, and I quickly came to understand just how limiting my four weeks of Spanish immersion classes would be. Although the classes did help my comprehension, trying to speak and retrieve the words I wanted to express felt nearly impossible. I decided the best thing to do was just to let Pablo do the talking, and to my great relief, he graciously switched to speaking English.

Pablo shared how he came to be a retired shaman. As an adolescent, he had been very sick with a heart ailment that allopathic medicine could not cure. He was ultimately healed of his heart troubles, and his sister of her debilitating hepatitis, by the shamanistic practice of *vegetalismo* (plant healing), which led him to feel called to become a healer. I would come to learn that the calling for most healers rarely came as a gentle tap, but rather as a powerful pounding and subsequent blowing-open in the form of some type of crisis—be it physical, emotional, psychological, or spiritual.

Pablo began to work with the sacred medicine ayahuasca, a complex hallucinogenic plant brew imbibed as a sacred practice for healing and spiritual growth. He explained that under the influence of ayahuasca, the shaman is not only transported to spiritual realms and higher levels of consciousness, but is also given lessons and specific information from the plant spirits on the medicinal uses of various plants. Pablo became known as a powerful healer and began to paint his ayahuasca visions in hopes of sharing the magic and mystery of his journeys with others. Perhaps out of humility, Pablo never told me what I would learn from Carina—that he was in fact a world-renowned artist, due to his visionary paintings, as well as a published author of *Ayahuasca Visions: The Religious Iconography of a Peruvian Shaman* and the recipient of the Global 500 peace prize from the United Nations Environment Programme.

As a shaman, Pablo experienced things that he said were too terrifying to discuss. It was the only occasion during our time together when

I saw the smile leave his face. Pablo explained that just as there are good shamans, there is also a dark side to that world. Helping people who had been victims of sorcerers, whose intentions are to harm rather than to heal, put Pablo in the line of fire. Fearing for his life, he decided to give up his shamanistic practice to focus on social work and being an advocate for the preservation of rain forest life. He started the Usko Ayar school in his own home, taking in children and offering a safe house where they could have community, focused attention, and creative expression. It was also a way for the children to develop self-esteem and pride in the riches of their culture and environment. The program includes a two-week excursion into the rain forest in which Pablo passes on his knowledge of the medicinal and spiritual value of the rain forest and of nature. He invited me to join them when I could return to Peru.

"When I look at how a child paints," Pablo told me, "it tells me what is happening for them, the state of their mind or heart, if they are troubled or at peace." He pointed to a heart-shaped blossom with a pink glow, depicted in one of his paintings, and said, "This plant, which cures heart ailments, is now extinct. But when you look at its essence in this painting, you can receive its healing energy."

"It sounds to me like you're not retired at all," I said. "You just changed the way you administer your medicine." He just grinned.

We parted, vowing to see each other again soon. We exchanged gifts. Pablo gave me a bracelet of seeds made by the Shipibo people and a pot painted in their community's patterns—physical expressions of the song lines of the *icaros,* sacred chants sung during the ayahuasca ceremonies. The song-line patterns serve as musical notation does in sheet music. I gave him a faceted quartz crystal, something I thought may symbolize the clarity and power of his heart. Okay, it was a little New Age, but it wasn't something he could easily get in his neck of the woods. As I started for the door, he handed me one more surprise—a stack of paintings from some of the instructors and students, and mixed among them, one of his originals.

We wrapped up our time at Usko Ayar, and the following day began our exploration upriver. The mode of transportation was a small open metal motorboat. I had boat envy as I watched others passing us in the *peke peke* (pronounced "pehkeh, pehkeh"), canoe taxis equipped with a motor and an awning for protection from rain and sun. Despite the diminutive size of our boat, getting out of the port was no small feat. First we boarded the boat at the dock and had to ride to the boathouse of the Tarzan Boat Company, which was floating freely in the middle of the harbor. Then we did a test run circling around the harbor to see if the boat could carry all of us plus the cargo load. It turned out we were too much for the little motor, so it was back to the boathouse. Once fitted with a more powerful motor, we headed back to the Tarzan house so the man in charge could approve. Then off to pick up the inspector, only to realize, discouragingly, that we were taking him back to Tarzan house so he could inspect the boat and motor. Because the Ucayali River is a busy trade route, there seemed to be a boathouse for every type of commerce. We visited the candy store boathouse and then the gas barge. After the forty-five minutes it took us to finally get out of port, my booty was already sore, and the imminent sunburn began making its presence known. And we had another hour and forty minutes before we'd get to our destination. Again I was reminded that in this type of travel, patience is not a virtue but rather a survival skill. Plus, I was in no mood to complain. The detours were all part of the ride, and that little metal boat managed to chug upriver with 1,500 pounds of people and cargo.

We had only three days to visit several villages for the purpose of exploring their sustainability practices, preservation of traditions, medicinal plants, and openness to the children's cultural exchange program. As we rode upriver, we passed riverbanks thick with foliage. One of the high points of the ride was getting a close-up glimpse of freshwater dolphins.

When we landed at the first village on our itinerary, Nueva Betania, a man and his pet baby monkey greeted us. As we made our way toward the village schoolhouse, a fifteen-minute walk from the landing, children were peering out of the windows of huts. The brave ones came out to follow us. Most of the villagers were relaxing on hammocks or in their homes, for we'd arrived at the hottest part of the day when it is wise and a traditional practice to take a siesta. I felt like an invader disrupting this traditional designated quiet time. All the gear I had so painstakingly gathered—my big boots, long-sleeved shirt, long pants, raingear—seemed like overkill on seeing how free and cool the villagers were, barefoot and lightly clothed.

Our main task here was to meet with the village fathers to propose our cultural exchange program ideas. Ambassador Bobby made our job easier by being completely himself and engaging the kids along the way. He handed out gifts of pencils, paper, and stickers and took Polaroid pictures of various kids, directing them and setting up their poses. He'd then present the kids with photos of themselves, which brought smiles and shrieks of laughter. One little girl overcame her extreme bashfulness—"I want to see the little white man," she'd announced—and approached us to give Bobby a small clay pot painted with the traditional Shipibo stair-step patterns. While Bobby and the kids, now numbering about fifty, played with a toy globe ball outside the schoolhouse, we four women met with the village chief and all the men of the village. Although it was a bit intimidating to be in front of the classroom facing all these men and their questions, it felt great to have such an open dialogue. It didn't take long for us to come to an agreement to explore the possibilities of what cultural exchange would mean to the kids of this village and those in the United States. Our meeting closed with the children of Nueva Betania singing us a traditional song, and Bobby singing a solo back to them.

This pretty planet
Spinning through space
You're a garden
You're a harbor
You're a holy place
Golden sun going down
Gentle blue giant
Spin us around
All through the night
Safe till the morning light

The little white man and his mother headed back to their home in San Francisco, California, while Elsa, Carina, and I headed to the village of San Francisco, another Shipibo community along the Ucayali River. San Francisco village was more "industrialized" than Nueva Betania. Every hut had a solar panel, which could run three fluorescent lights or a small television. There were solar-powered street lamps, a community cellular phone, and a lake where the villagers raised about thirty species of fish. We learned from the village leaders that once, after tourism became more prevalent in the area, the villagers tried to sell their goods to outsiders. They discovered that being dependent on external sources for their livelihood put them at greater risk than being self-sustaining. The village leaders then decided that they would return to raising their own food as they had done traditionally, continuing to integrate new technologies to improve their lives, and selling only the additional goods that they didn't need to outsiders. This proved to be a model that allowed the villagers to be independent as well as to prosper from some outside influences.

Wellington, a.k.a. Wonder Hands, who had spent two years teaching painting in San Francisco, was our guide. He introduced us to his godmother, Herlinda, whose family adopted Wellington during his stay. It turned out that Herlinda was the leader of the women's council and she and her husband were the village shamans. She talked to us about "women's medicine," part of which was the painting of the traditional Shipibo geometric patterns on cloth. The reddish-orange dye for the background color of the cloth was derived from the soaking of a local tree bark, while the black pigment for the actual patterns and designs was made with clay from the highlands.

Herlinda sang a song over the bark mixture and told us that this allowed the spirits to give her visions of the patterns she was to paint. Then she showed us finished cloth made by her children and gifted us small patches painted by her six-year-old granddaughter that were amazingly complex in design. When she showed us the cloth painted by her son, designed not with the traditional geometric patterns but rather with animals and plants, she said with pride that this was evidence of Wellington's teaching and influence. As we left Herlinda's home, she honored

Elsa, Carina, and me with an invitation to return for teachings on the craft of cloth painting and the medicine that women weave through it. She then demonstrated by running her fingers along the patterns and singing a sacred chant as the lines dictated the lyrics and notes, explaining that the patterns were the physical manifestations of the icaros, the sacred healing songs.

Enrique, the village shaman and Herlinda's husband, was away, so his son, Alberto, took us on a tour of the medicinal garden. We touched, smelled, and tasted various plants. Elsa, the ever-curious ethnobotanist, took specimens of every plant and carefully wrapped each in newspaper. Trying not to disrupt Alberto's tour, I attempted to subtly slap myself as droves of mosquitoes attacked me with vehemence. Alberto finally cut a twig from a tree, broke it to extract a white milky substance, and instructed me to rub it on my bites. Ah, sweet relief. He then proceeded to show us the various plants that he used to make the ayahuasca hallucinogenic brew and invited us to return to participate in a ceremony once his father returned. Although I understood his offering was a great honor, I had mixed feelings about trying such a brew, as part of me felt like it was somehow akin to cheating. Wasn't the way to enlightenment and spiritual realms supposed to take years of study, practice, and meditation? Yet I also wanted to respect that this was the pathway for these healers and the tradition for many of the people of the Amazon. I made a note at least to consider it in the future.

Leaving the Ucayali and Pucallpa area was just as hectic as our landing. On our way to the airport for our flight to Iquitos, the biggest Peruvian Amazon city in the northeast region of Loreto, our taxi suffered a flat tire. We had to run the last half mile to the airport. Now, a half mile may not seem like a long way, but having to schlep a backpack, camera bag, and duffle bag in the heat and humidity really upped the ante. So many times during these travels I wished I had been a workout queen back home, a sprightly in-shape Wonder Woman ready to glide with grace through these types of situations. Nevertheless, sweaty and unglamorous, we did make it on time, with me taking up the rear and vowing to do serious cardiovascular and strength training once I got home.

We were picked up at the Iquitos airport and whisked to the lodge offices, where we filled out paperwork. We were then taken on a boat upriver to the lodge that was closest to the rain forest canopy. When we arrived, Elsa, Carina, and I went into a bit of culture shock. After having spent time in remote villages, being at a brand-new lodge with air-conditioned rooms, a bar, a pool with an artificial waterfall, a whirlpool and a slide, and resort prices was discombobulating. We were matched with a guide who acted like it was his job to talk us out of everything we wanted to do. We believed that the owners of these facilities must have been used to planning and controlling everything for tourists who didn't want to think for themselves, and Carina and I felt as if our parents had sent us to summer camp and the lodge personnel were our chaperones.

It was only because of our strong desire to walk among the treetops of the rain forest canopy that we agreed to put up with the unfriendly service and price gouging. We found out on arrival that it would cost us an extra $120 per person to tour the canopy—a total of $360. Elsa discovered that hiring a local boat would have cost us just $2. After our initial grumbling, the girls and I decided we needed an attitude adjustment. Reluctantly, we went for a swim in the pool and worked at not being judgmental. We tried to make ourselves feel better by saying things like, "Well, at least this place draws people to learn about the rain forest who may not ordinarily do it," or "Maybe they're paying the local employees really well."

The next day, we were headed to the canopy and decided we should comply with the lodge's rules of booking every activity through them. On the way, we insisted on stopping at one of the villages along the river to make contact with a schoolteacher about the cultural exchange program. The Palmeras community was still a bit flooded, so in order to get to the schoolhouse, we had to roll up our pants, take off our shoes, and wade through knee-high puddles. There was something so freeing about being barefoot in the mud, other than for the small threat of exposure to fungus and bacteria. Elsa tried to make light of it, telling me that everyone who spends time mucking around in rain forest terrain will eventually get a fungus, so I should just accept that. She didn't realize she was talking to someone who refuses to get pedicures at nail salons (even though most are run by my own countrywomen) to avoid such things.

At the schoolhouse all the children were receiving their school supplies. Because of flood season, their school year runs from May to December, when the water has receded and the mud has dried. The school director was very interested in the cultural exchange program because he felt the village's proximity to the lodge had already exposed the kids to people of other cultures. He wanted to strengthen the children's pride in their own Yagua culture.

When we waded back to the boat landing, we discovered that the boat that had dropped us off at the village, the one that was supposed to take us to the canopy, had been sent away to pick up other lodge guests. Our surly guide, whom I'd privately named the No Man because he seemed to relish not accommodating us, said it was because we didn't return to the boat on time, so we'd have to wait for the next boat to come along. Hmm ... and this was supposedly a private charter that cost us an extra $360. The mix of No Man's passive-aggressive behavior and the lodge exploiting us got me steamed. I said my piece to No Man, who just looked at me and shrugged his shoulders. From that point on, we deemed the lodge Exploit-ama, a play on its similar-sounding name.

I told myself I had to get back to a place of peace or I would not be in the right state of mind to experience the magic of the rain forest canopy. I said a prayer to find compassion in my heart. Then something magical happened. The closer we got to the canopy, the nicer No Man got. As he guided us at record speed toward the canopy sky bridges, it became apparent to me that this man loved the rain forest and hated his job. Being here was his reward for putting up with demanding tourists. It turned out he earned only a paltry salary of $100 per month, less than the cost of one night's stay at the lodge.

To reach the series of sky bridges, we first had to climb up a ladder to the starter platform. From there we began to cross the rope and metal bridges two at a time. Elsa got paired with Carina, and I partnered up with the guide formerly known as No Man. These sky bridges led to twelve different platforms, each at various heights among the treetops. Elsa's face was beaming as she took in the view that reminded her of why she spends most of her life trudging through jungles and putting up with tropical diseases and afflictions. As one of the warriors fighting to save the rain forest, its cultures, and its medicinal plants, she had spent her life in the trenches of this war. At last she was now able to rise above and remember the beauty of her work and dreams.

As our tour was ending and we approached the last of the sky bridges, it began to pour. Rather than put our rain gear on, we all opted to get wet and run wildly through the jungle. It felt freeing, cleansing, and the hard rains chased the mosquitoes away. Unfortunately, it also washed away the bug repellent from our skin, and as soon as the rains stopped, the swarms returned and mercilessly began devouring us. From heavenly heights to the bottom of the food chain, I realized what bit me worse than the mosquitoes was the adventure bug.

CHAPTER 3

Meeting My Guides

San Jose, California (Meeting the Mentor)

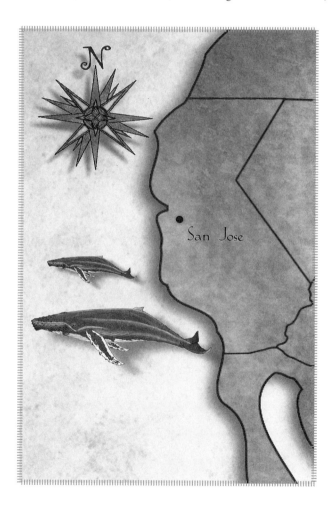

My first taste of adventure and initial foray into the world of shamanism confirmed that my dream was actually becoming a reality. I returned to Seattle more determined than ever to find a way to continue. I needed some time to seek additional funding, but in the meantime I could continue my research. As luck would have it, it was during this period that I was given a special opportunity to meet a spiritual healer from my home country who also happened to be part of my own family and who lived just a short flight away in San Jose, California.

I'd previously heard whispers about Aunty Lien, a much sought-after spiritual healer in Vietnam. I say "whispers" because people of a certain educated class in my culture tend to steer clear of anything that may make them appear superstitious or unrefined—a holdover from colonization. Aunty Lien was my aunt by marriage, my half-brother's wife's mother, to be exact. I'd recently reconnected with my elder half-brother, Thanh. Upon learning of my spiritual seeking, he shared stories about his mother-in-law's abilities to heal, to see spirits, and to foretell the future. I was anxious to get to know her for what she might be able to offer my project's exploration of healing practices and spiritual traditions, but I found I had other, stronger motives for connecting with her as well.

Even though it had been months since I'd left my teacher's tutelage, if I allowed myself to think of her for too long, I would still experience a sinking in my chest and tightness in my stomach. An internal diatribe of self-flagellation for my stupidity, naïveté, and gullibility would then follow. I found myself still seeking a mentor—a light that could pull me out of these dark places. I secretly hoped I might find in Aunty Lien a mentor with integrity who would be a force of goodness that could blast away the traces of my previous teacher's treachery.

The more Thanh told me about Aunty Lien, however, another, more compelling reason to spend time with her emerged: she was apparently able to communicate with my deceased father's spirit. My father, a colonel in the South Vietnamese army, was diagnosed with liver cancer while I was in my mother's womb. Despite receiving a prognosis that he had only six more months, he managed to live until I was two years old. Like most people who lose a parent at a young age, what I knew of my father came from other people's stories, which tended to mythologize as they eulogized. I'd heard from men who served under him that he was a beloved and well-respected leader. I'd heard from family friends that he not only had a brilliant military mind, having been trained by both the French and Americans, but also a poet's heart. I'd heard from family members that he was charismatic, kind, and brutally handsome. And from my mother, I could hear the longing for him and the chiding of him as she described how he could sweep women off their feet on the dance floor, serenade them into submission, and employ the most exquisite French in his elegant cursive to express his ardor. The photos of his funeral with full military honors and a procession of hundreds marching through the streets of Saigon, the framed black-and-whites of him in uniform looking like a movie star, and the love letters he'd written to my mother only helped to ingrain in my mind the romantic image of a bona fide renaissance man.

Although Thanh and I shared the same father, we had lived very separate lives after his death and since fleeing the war. While my mom, siblings, and I left after the Tet Offensive of 1968 and headed to France, Thanh escaped the year before Saigon fell. The rest of his family joined him in Hawaii in 1975 and they later settled in San Jose. In 1990, Aunty Lien and her husband were finally able to leave Vietnam and join Thanh and his wife, Annie, bringing with them a surprise—our father's ashes. Thanh was nine years old when our father passed, but it wasn't until he held that box of ashes, twenty-five years later, that he finally wept for his loss. He later told me that it was visitations from my father's spirit coming to him in his dreams and through Aunty Lien that inspired him to connect with me and my siblings.

Thanh warned me that Aunty Lien didn't like to talk much about spiritual matters or her healing work, so we'd have to approach the subject with great respect, which in the Vietnamese way meant allowing her to bring it up. She had wanted to leave that part of her life behind when she came to the United States. Now a retired healer, she was happy to care only for her husband, daughter, son-in-law, and two grandsons rather than the droves of people who used to come to her seeking help. Because she was now leading a "normal" life, she relished doing the simple things— cooking for her family, babysitting the grandkids, praying, and working in her garden. The other reason for her reticence to talk openly about her healing work was the depth of the stigma left from the influences of French colonization, Catholic conversion, and American assimilation, for it led many Vietnamese people to see believing in such healing traditions as not only ignorant but even shameful or evil. I would find this to be a common theme among people of cultures in transition. In order to assimilate into a modern world, many feel they must reject and vilify what has been a part of their culture's cosmology for centuries.

Annie, my sister-in-law, explained that she had never actually seen her mother practicing her healing work because the "strange happenings" did not begin until after Annie was sent to the United States. Her parents remained in Vietnam unable to escape for fifteen years, and she only knew what she'd heard from former patients and from her father, who was still uncomfortable that his quiet wife changed during that time into something he could not fully understand. To him, it seemed that his wife got the calling from the spirit world and overnight she was no longer just his. Suddenly, they had people lined up outside their home in Saigon seeking help with illnesses of the body, mind, and spirit.

Aunty Lien did her healing work as a medium or trance channel. Unlike a shaman, who leaves his or her body and travels to the spiritual realms to retrieve healing information and visions, a medium brings spirits through the body to give healing touch, medicinal advice, and prophetic information. Aunty Lien would later clarify that she was not possessed like people who are taken over by evil spirits or lost souls, but rather her "seat" was reserved only for being in service to high deities or saints, as she would call them, such as Quan Am (the Vietnamese name for the Buddhist goddess of compassion). Annie admitted to me that she sometimes heard her mother talking to someone, perhaps the spirits, when she thought no one else was around.

The first time I met Aunty Lien was not actually planned. As part of Thanh's family reconnection efforts, I'd been invited to a birthday party for one of our mutual cousins. I flew to San Jose from Seattle, eager to get reacquainted with that part of my family. As I was chatting with other partygoers, Annie approached me and said she felt compelled to take me to her mother right then. It was great timing for me, since I had been thinking what a shame it would be for me to be in San Jose and not meet Aunty Lien. But I was willing to honor tradition and wait to be invited. When Annie let Thanh know what we were up to, he looked at us with a startled expression. "Right now?" he asked. "You're going to leave in the middle of this party?" It wasn't lost on me that our departure was not only awkward, but also bad etiquette. She shrugged, smiled, gave an apologetic look. "We'll be back," she said. As Annie drove us, she said to me, "I can't explain why I feel I have to take you to my mother right *now.*"

When we arrived, Aunty Lien was in the kitchen cooking, and she seemed happy and not at all surprised to see us. Annie had just started to introduce us when suddenly Aunty Lien's face shifted from open and friendly to serious and focused. She gave me a piercing look, rushed toward me, and then vigorously hugged me, caressed my face, repeatedly cupping it with her hands, and then gave me a series of Vietnamese kisses on my cheeks. A Vietnamese kiss is a very intimate act of affection done with the nose rather than the lips. It consists of strong quick inhalations through the nostrils creating a vacuum effect and suction sound when released. It is as if we are taking in the essence of those we love with this gesture. Being on the receiving end of such a kiss feels sweeter than words can describe. Whenever I unleash the nose kiss onto my nieces and nephews or unsuspecting American friends, it always evokes shrieks and giggles. But, this reception from Aunty Lien was unusual because we had never met; the usual etiquette would have been my bowing to her and at the most her taking my hand or patting the inside of my forearm. In fact, even receiving a pat on the shoulders or back from an elder would be considered a very significant demonstration of love and affection.

Aunty Lien took me by the hand into her dining room, and we sat facing each other. She then began to speak to me in a mix of French and English. "Oh, my child! *Quel plaisir de te voir!* It's so good to see you." As she looked me up and down, she then began to weep. She gently stroked my face and continued, *"Ma petite fille,* my little girl, I'm so sorry that I left you when you were so little, *si petite."* Tears were now streaming down her face. I looked at Annie, who was standing next to us, stunned.

After my initial shock, what was being said began to land. It suddenly dawned on me that I knew this person who was talking to me. Aunty Lien continued, *"Mais, tu sais comme je t'aime?* But you must know how much I love you. *Je serais toujours près de toi.* I will always be near you. You must remember that. I love you so; *je t'aime beaucoup ma petite fille."* It was my turn to weep now, for these were the words I had longed to hear from a father who had previously only lived in my imagination. To hear them coming through a source outside myself, and actually feeling the love projected at me, was beyond any experience I could have imagined. Aunty Lien suddenly got quiet. Before I could say what flashed into my mind—*Wait! I'm not ready for you to go*—I knew it was over. He was gone.

Aunty Lien rubbed her face and reverted to Vietnamese. "What happened? What did I say?" I learned that it was common for a medium not to remember what was said through them while they are channeling because of the trancelike state they go into. When Annie described what she'd seen and heard, Aunty Lien looked at me and sighed, "Ah … your father! He's so persistent." Apparently, his spirit had been visiting her in dreams asking to let him come through her to see me. She explained that he told her I would be coming to see her soon. He'd pleaded with her, saying that because he'd died when I was two, there were things he needed to tell me. Father had asked her for just five minutes. Aunty Lien said, "I told him, 'you know it's not up to me. My seat is only for saints and goddesses—not just regular spirits like you.' Oh, but he wouldn't give up, and he kept coming and coming for seven nights now." Exasperated and exhausted from his disrupting her sleep, she finally agreed that she would let him through if he petitioned the high deities, who would decide whether or not they would let him use her, their seat, to see me. Aunty Lien smiled and added, "That father of yours can charm anyone to get his way—even the saints."

On our way back to the party, Annie told me, "You know, my mom doesn't speak French, and her English is not that good. Your father must have done that so you would know it was really him. And, you know, my mother never touches and hugs people like that—not even me." Annie explained that despite her mother's extreme love for her daughter, it was not her nature to express her love and affection so physically or with such strong verbal declarations. It was still very new for Annie to see her mother in this light, but what she had just witnessed made her mother's gift undeniable. For those five minutes, her mother had not been her mother. We sat quietly for the rest of the drive, her processing the idea of her mother turning into another person and me processing the idea that the person her mother turned into was the father I'd lost thirty-five years earlier. Those five minutes with him were a precious gift to last a lifetime, yet the more I clutched to hold onto them, the more they escaped my grasp. I found myself thinking of all the things I'd wished I'd asked or said to him and running his words over and over in my mind to be sure I hadn't missed one drop of his presence. And occasionally I glanced over at Annie and felt relieved that her look of shock was evidence that I hadn't imagined it all.

Back at my condo that hovered atop columns over the shoreline of Lake Washington, the agitated water rhythmically pounding against my building's underbelly, I looked out at the drizzling gray and felt a loneliness that seeped through to my bones. I couldn't help but fixate on what sweet succor it was for me to experience my father's spirit by the grace of Aunty Lien's spiritual gifts. My Pavlovian response was to try to return to the same source in search of that deep sense of comfort for what ailed me most when I was still and not busying myself. I was seeking to somehow soothe

the anguish I was still feeling over my botched spiritual education. The damage done by what occurred between my teacher and me was profound, but at the top of the list of worst things for me, an Asian American with immigrant overachiever syndrome, was the sense of failure. In my family, getting an A on schoolwork stood for "acceptable," while a B stood for "bad," and an F was basically "fatal." In my fantasy world I wanted to proceed as if I'd withdrawn from a class I'd signed up for because of a bad professor. I convinced myself somewhere along the way that I'd be able to retake the courses with more competent, caring instructors in hopes of salvaging my GPA.

I found myself hoping to be able to broach with Aunty Lien the subject of her possibly becoming my new mentor. Perhaps under the auspices of research for my project, it would be easier to engage her in a deeper dialogue. So, I was more than eager when Thanh invited me for another visit a few weeks later. It would give me a chance to hang out with him and Annie and get to know my two nephews better. We'd also planned to visit the cemetery that now housed my father's ashes, the physical remnants of his spirit. Aunty Lien and her husband would be there as well; they spent weekdays at Thanh's and weekends at their own apartment.

The second time I saw Aunty Lien, greeting me with a smile and a nod from Thanh's kitchen, she was not larger than life, as I'd remembered her. She was her diminutive quiet self, standing at the stove at just under five feet tall with her salt-and-pepper hair in a chignon, making lunch for all of us. It seemed we would have a rather normal visit this time. As proper protocol dictated, no one would mention what happened during our first meeting.

Aunty Lien beckoned me to step out to the backyard with her. She picked herbs from her garden and proudly pointed out the abundant growth of bottle gourd that sprung from the ground and hung from vines on a trellis. My mouth watered at the prospect of the delicious prawn soup that would be made with this bounty. Aunty Lien then said she wanted to show me something special. She led me to a small metal tool shed and slid open the doors. Rather than finding the expected lawnmower, weed whacker, or hedge clippers, I saw a delightful ensemble of spiritual tools.

It was dark inside save for the small blinking Christmas lights that were draped around a cloth backdrop and three electric candles with bulbs acting as flames. Leaning against the cloth in the center of a shelf was a framed photo of Quan Am riding the holy dragon, next to her a statue of Buddha. On the shelf one level down was a stand with three incense sticks, to the left of which was a bowl of mangoes and to the right a bowl of persimmons that served as offerings. Sprinkled among those items were several vases filled with colorful plastic flowers. Aunty Lien said that when she stayed with her daughter's family, she lit incense and prayed every morning at this sacred altar. At her home, she had two altars facing each other, one that is a mini version of the one I was looking at and the other one adorned with a cross and two angel figurines surrounding a statue of the Virgin Mary. "Quan Am and Mother Mary are two of my sponsors, so I have to pay respect and pray to them both," she explained. A sponsor is a spiritual guide who takes a healer under his or her wing, protecting and empowering them.

In my mind, the idea that Aunty Lien could connect me with some powerful sponsors from the spirit world to protect and empower me was like a bright beacon of hope. Beyond the feelings of betrayal and failure, I was at times plagued with an uneasy feeling of being unprotected in the spiritual sense since the fallout with my former teacher. Because I did not detect darkness until I was enveloped by it, I felt somehow unsafe to continue exploring the mysteries of the metaphysical realms without mentors or guides. Although I did escape from an unhealthy situation, I was far from unscathed.

I didn't realize it then, but Aunty Lien had already begun to teach me. In sharing these small intimacies, she was inviting me into her world and reminding me of the value of patience and respect for elders, allowing them to bestow upon me the gifts they were ready to share. In my culture, it is not for the junior to ask for what they need or desire, but rather it is expected that an elder will know and have the wisdom to decide what is appropriate to offer and when to offer it. This renewed understanding set the tone for how I would approach every healer and elder I would meet on my journeys to follow. It was a delicate repatterning of my Western upbringing and entertainment business and corporate-America training, in which I was rewarded for being direct, cutting to the chase to get things done and to get ahead.

While the soup was simmering, Aunty Lien sat with Annie, Thanh, and me, and over steaming tea told us about bringing our father's ashes to the United States. In 1990 she'd received permission to emigrate from Vietnam to the United States. It was then that my father's spirit began to appear to her in her dreams, although they were never acquainted when he was living. "Your father was so stubborn," she said, smiling. "He kept appearing to me and asking me to bring him closer to his family." At that time, she told him firmly that she was not at the bidding of restless spirits, so just as he had to acquire permission to come through her to see me the last time she and I were together, he had to petition her spiritual sponsors then to have this request sanctioned. Apparently, my father's power of persuasion and spiritual sway were very effective. A relative brought the ashes to her in Saigon, and together, Aunty Lien, her husband, and that box made it out of Vietnam and through a treacherous boat ride, refugee processing camps, and sniffing security dogs. During the long boat trip, she would talk to her suitcase that held father's ashes and make him offerings of egg and fruit. "I'm doing this for you, so please protect us. Help us get to America safely." She giggled when she recalled that at times her fellow passengers gave her looks of pity as if she were a crazy old woman.

I realized what a coup it was for my father's spirit to be able to harness Aunty Lien's privileges for his agendas when she explained why it never should have happened. At the time that he began to appear to her, she had just completed her long, arduous process of being released from her duties as a healer. In order to be given a sort of early retirement, she had to petition for three years so she could, as she put it, "give back her seat." In those three years, she and a group of her supporters had nightly rituals of prayer and 108 prostrations before seven different deities. Within that time, she also had to make difficult pilgrimages to ten sacred pagodas throughout Vietnam, reciting prayers all along the way. She got her retirement approval from the spiritual authorities around the same time that she received approval from the government authorities to leave Vietnam.

"So, you see," Aunty Lien concluded, "once I gave back my seat, I was supposed to stop channeling and using my gifts." But, she clarified that although she was now retired, her body is still preserved and could be used once in a great while in special cases—kind of like entering the military reserves after retirement from regular duty. Although my hopes of her potentially becoming my teacher began to fade as she talked, there was still the "special case" possibility. After all, my father was able to pull that card more than once.

When it was time for the actual meal, just as we were about to dig into the appetizers of cold salad rolls—rice paper wraps filled with shrimp, pork, herbs, and rice vermicelli—Aunty Lien abruptly got up from the table and went down the hall. When she returned, her face appeared freshly washed, as there was moisture around the edges of her hairline. She seemed some-what distant and somber as she sat down. Then her eyelids drooped a bit and she turned toward me. I had a feeling in that moment that my sweet, gentle Aunty Lien had left the building and someone else was at the mic.

A stream of Vietnamese words, thrown at me like flying daggers, came too fast for me to dodge or decipher on my own. This was definitely not going to be the touchy-feely experience I'd had with my father's spirit. I looked at Thanh for backup. It somehow comforted me that he looked as astonished as I felt. "She says you're stubborn and you're wasting your gifts. You can hear the spirits, but you won't listen," he nervously translated. Aunty Lien then stood, moved away from the table, and started kicking her legs and flailing her arms. The movements were rigid, as if she were about to do the Robot or moonwalk. This hit me at once as freaky and funny. "She says she wants to kick you and throw you out," he continued. I shot him a "what the hell?" look, and he replied with one that said, "How should I know?" while continuing to calmly translate. "Uh ... she says they want to take away your gifts because you are not using them properly." As she continued, Thanh explained, "They are going to have some kind of a meeting now." Aunty Lien was quiet for a moment. When she did speak again it was with a more gentle tone.

It was explained that my spiritual posse had gathered for a meeting to decide whether or not I should be allowed to retain my healing gifts. It turned out that my biggest sponsor was Mother Mary herself, who stepped forward just in the nick of time. Apparently she argued that despite my being young and stubborn, I had a good heart, good intention, and strong past karma of helping others, so she proposed to the other goddesses and saints that I be put on probation rather than having my gifts stripped from me. Once that was settled, just as she had after my father's spirit left her, Aunty Lien rubbed her face, opened her eyes wide, and asked what had happened. When we told her, she chuckled at times and made comments like, "Oh, that was the strict one. She can give you life or take it away," and "Ah, yes, the thousand-armed goddess," and "It's so good that your major sponsor is Mother Mary. Yes, that's very good."

As I marveled at the contrast between this soft-spoken, kind lady and the wrathful deities that had come through her, I found myself not only feeling a bit shell-shocked, but also embarrassed and angry. In the first place, I was mad at myself for being the idiot who had naively wished to connect with powerful sponsors, and second, I was mad at these gal guides who were supposed to empower and protect me, and who instead berated me in a manner I had not experienced since my early days on a live television crew, when I was forced to endure the rants of stressed-out directors, producers, and "talent." In truth, I guess I felt hurt because I expected these saints to be nurturing and supportive, and instead I got whacked while I was already down. It seemed unfair somehow.

Everyone tried to act normally after that, but the quiet in which we finished our meal was palpable. I tried to focus on the delicious food, but found myself talking back to the goddesses in my head. *What do you mean misusing my gifts? How am I going to be tested, and how do I pass this friggin' test? What the heck am I supposed to do with this kind of vague message? Why did you have to be so nasty? Since when is being stubborn such a big crime?* Okay, so I did what any pouting child would do after a major wrist-slapping—I got defensive. I understood that I was reluctant to use my gifts after what happened with my teacher, but I felt erring on the side of caution was a good thing. And, since I couldn't yet trust myself, how could I know I would not turn out to be like her? But my sponsors must have known how well I respond to reverse psychology. A sure way to get me to do anything is to tell me I can't. Somehow, their threatening to take away my gifts made me want to fight for them, to explore them fully so that I'd know what I was in danger of losing, and in doing so at least I would be the one to choose, rather than have that choice made for me. I decided that evening that whatever test they were going to throw my way, I was damned determined to pass with flying colors. *I'll show you stubborn.*

The third time I saw Aunty Lien, she must have understood my struggle with the messages that came through her during our last visit because she sat me down for a heart to heart. She generously shared her own story with me, perhaps to give me greater perspective. The goddesses first came to her in dreams and told her she had to accept their command to help others. At first she refused to do it. She asked, "Why me?" and "How would that work?" They told her she had been chosen for her purity of heart and maturity. They would borrow her body from the chest up and only three of them would be working through her and guiding her to help others. They would place two angels, one on each shoulder, to protect her.

When they first tried to come into Aunty Lien's body, she fought to block them. She said the pressure was immense and it felt like someone was breaking her neck. The goddesses said to her, "Why are you being so stubborn? This is an honor and order you should accept." I smiled at hearing that I wasn't the only one who had been charged with the crime of stubbornness. She really didn't want to commit and submit to their demands, but was curious to see what would happen, so she agreed to stop resisting and give it a try. Aunty Lien was scared as one of the goddesses then entered her body. She felt overcome with extreme fatigue and lost consciousness. As she came to, she saw her husband and neighbors tending to her and heard a voice saying, "Don't worry, this was just the first time. From now on it will be smoother and you'll be okay." It took her a moment to realize that strange voice was coming from within her.

Aunty Lien did eventually allow herself to be a vehicle of healing for these deities and was fully initiated, receiving a seal from her spiritual sponsors. This seal was a symbol, and appeared as a red cross on the palms of her hands, remaining there until she officially retired. One of her first healings was curing someone of chronic headaches by a laying on of hands and pressing the seal to the forehead. From that simple case she went on to more complicated ones. Another patient, who suffered from listlessness, constant vomiting, and an inability to eat was unresponsive to treatment by doctors at the hospital. While channeling, Aunty Lien could see in her mind's eye that this patient had lost a son and a sister and was being haunted by their spirits. Apparently, she had not done the proper ceremonies and prayers to honor and release their souls and they were trying to get this woman's attention. Aunty Lien performed an exorcism and the patient's symptoms cleared. As word spread of Aunty Lien's abilities to cure illnesses, to predict the future, and to perform exorcisms, people began to line up in front of her home seeking healing or divine guidance. At times, she would receive a message from the spirit world to go to a patient, and she would have to drop whatever she was doing and follow those orders. She said this was very hard on her husband, as it made life with her very unpredictable, not to mention that what she did frightened him. Yet, she stayed firm in her commitment.

Aunty Lien then turned to me and said, "You are young, my child. You have the gift, but it's not yet solid. You can't decide which way to go. You're restless—always going here and there and everywhere. I can't tell you what to do, but if I were you, I would choose this path." Even with my aunty's stories and advice, I still only had a vague idea of what being on this path she referred to might mean. She went on to acknowledge that this would not be an easy choice, for I would have to be clean, pure of heart, and fully committed. Then she added, "And you have to be celibate." *Gulp!* Until that moment I thought I might have had half a chance to pass this test, but now the odds were definitely dismal, for although I was not planning to marry again, I was definitely not ready to give up my passion for carnal pleasures. I spent my formative years in France, after all, and absorbed the convention of cherishing scrumptious food, luscious wine, and juicy romance. Sigh. I finally mustered up the courage to ask Aunty Lien what had been so much on my mind: "If I choose to try and pass the test, will you teach me?" She gently replied, "I can't be your teacher because this is something that cannot be taught. You are chosen and you choose—or you don't."

It is really only now, in this moment, that I've come to understand why I had been scolded and put on probation then. It was not punishment, as I had long perceived it to be, but rather a ticket to ride for a while, to buy me more time to decide from a place of maturity and clarity.

Although she could not serve as my mentor and continue with me on my journey forward, Aunty Lien had laid the groundwork to help me prepare for what was to come. I understood that in telling me her stories, she was letting me know that she had been where I was and that where I might be going would not be easy street, but that the ride would be well worth the bumps. She also helped me to see that mentors and guides can come in all different forms—an aunt in flesh and blood, a father in spirit, or a goddess on a rampage. At that time, I could not have guessed that this would be our last visit, nor would I realize the prophetic nature of the dream I'd had sleeping in the room next to hers and its power to propel me forward, crossing the next threshold: *I am walking up a mountain trail. It is a difficult climb, and when I reach a plateau, I am relieved at finally having arrived. But I am told I had farther to go. I struggle, trekking ever higher. I reach the top of the mountain, and floating above me is the emanation of a Divine Goddess. She is dropping ancient texts to me, one page at a time. The pages float before me and then quickly fade out of view. I am told I must translate these secrets before they disappear. I begin to write as fast as I can.*

CHAPTER 4

Initiation

Hawaii (Crossing the Threshold, Part 1)

When I opened my eyes, what I saw before me was exactly the same as what I saw with my eyes closed—pure darkness, empty space—the void. Interestingly, this blackness did not evoke fear, but rather gave me a sense of being enveloped, held, and calmed.

We, the members of the Lucky Bastards Club (as the crew and I had taken to calling ourselves because we couldn't believe making a film while visiting paradise was our work), had crawled into the belly of Mother Earth by way of a lava tube and turned off our headlamps just for grins. Lava tubes are created when a lava flow cools on the surface, forming a solid crust above, while the hot river of molten rock continues beneath, leaving a tunnel once all the lava has been expelled. This was my first sense of what the native Hawaiians call the *mana* of the *aina,* the power of the land or of place.

The Big Island of Hawaii is home to the most active volcano in the world, with its goddess, Madame Pele, reigning supreme and expressing her power through fiery activity, leaving in its wake continuous transformation and tributaries from the inner realms to the outer world. Sitting in that stillness with only my own heartbeat and breathing as signs of life, I wondered if this is how it might feel to dwell in the womb of a mother who celebrated your being there. As we emerged from the cave, it felt like a rebirth, entering the world welcomed by soft light and a cool breeze—a sweet transition from dreaming to waking.

Aloha is a Hawaiian word that most people are familiar with. Although it is commonly used as a salutation, "hello" or "good-bye," to those who live the aloha spirit, it has a much deeper meaning. In speaking with the locals, we learned some of its many connotations—generosity, compassion, connecting to the breath of life, presence of spirit, embracing all as family—but the truest sense of the word that encompasses all the other meanings for aloha is love. And, it is not merely a word, but also a practice. A way of life.

I experienced the aloha spirit firsthand before I even knew I'd be going to Hawaii for this project. While doing my research on Hawaiian healing arts, I contacted Nancy Kahalewai, at the time the director and owner of the Academy of Massage in Hilo. She was writing a book on the traditional Hawaiian massage known as *lomilomi,* and was close to many of the Big Island's *kumu* (teachers). In that first conversation, once she understood my intention, she immediately asked, "Do you have any sponsors?" When I replied, "Not really; I'm just in the research phase," without hesitation, she offered, "Well, let me be your first sponsor! If you want to come here to learn about Hawaiian healing arts, I'll introduce you to all the healers and teachers I know, and you can stay in my house."

Nancy's initial offering of Aloha set the stage for all the serendipity and generous helping hands that would make an eleven-day trip to Hawaii possible. In Seattle, a mutual friend had introduced me to Cora, a fellow intrepid adventuress and producer, looking for a project to throw her heart into. After one conversation she was on board and within a few months had wrangled the funding to get us to the Big Island. We also had no problem convincing top-notch director of photography Joseph and sound guy Matt to join in. When we told them that the pay for our low-budget project would be their regular rates minus the fun factor, they both feared they would end up owing us money, but they were more than willing to take that risk.

Out of the fishbowl and into the ocean. I landed on the Big Island in search of spirituality and discovered sensuality, for here, the two are inseparable. When we landed and stepped off the airplane onto the tarmac of the open-air airport, I could feel the weight of the air on my skin. Driving along the highways and back roads, my eyes were inundated with the immense greens of the tropical rain forest and the blues of the ocean waters crashing along the deep black of lava rock beaches. The smells of tropical flowers and fruits would drift by in intoxicating waves. None of the healers or teachers Nancy introduced us to would allow us to simply observe what they had to share with me; they wanted to immerse us in the power of the physical elements of their paradise.

The first teacher we met was willing to speak with us on the condition that our initial meeting take place in the waters of a hot pond. A hot pond is a pool warmed by volcano-heated springs and cooled by ocean tides. Aunty Mahealani had a very special connection to this particular one, as her uncle and grandfather, along with the other men in their community, helped to build the Ahanalui hot pond by removing rocks, trees, and debris, making it a pool now big enough to do laps in. She wanted us to be cleansed by the sacred waters and explained one of the key concepts about the Big Island—it is a place where apparent opposites meet and must be accommodated as part of a whole. Accordingly, these hot ponds are one of the few places where Pele, the goddess of the volcano, and her rival, Nāmakaokahai, the goddess of the ocean, embrace each other and give those who swim in these waters access to two different realms at the same time. More than willing to accommodate her request, my fellow Lucky Bastards and I put the camera in a waterproof case, got into our suits, and hopped into the soothing waters of the hot pond, experiencing the luscious embrace of two goddesses.

Aunty Mahealani refers to the hot pond as her office, and it is her favorite place from which to teach Hawaiian culture and her take on spirituality. She calls her teachings *ho'oponopono ke ala*. Aunty explained that *ho'oponopono* commonly means to right a wrong and was traditionally used as a method of conflict resolution, cleansing, and forgiveness. It was a process of mediation in which injured parties could express their grievances to the community leader while agreeing to put aside their differences per the leader's remediation recommendation. Once the parties in conflict were in agreement and compliance, the issue was never to be spoken of again. But in Aunty Mahealani's understanding of things, the deeper ancient roots of this practice are based on the greater teachings of Hawaiian spirituality, in which there is no damnation or original sin, so the words really mean, "to make what is right, more right," or "what is good *(pono)*, even better (double pono)." In adding *ke ala* to her form of Ho'oponopono, it means the way or the path to making right.

I noted that most of the students who had accompanied Aunty to her office were not of Hawaiian culture. She explained that what she is teaching was once *kapu* (forbidden), to be discussed and kept only within the family for fear of retribution by the outsiders who made speaking the Hawaiian language and practicing Hawaiian traditions a punishable crime. But now, with the resurgence of pride in their culture, many Hawaiians have lifted the kapu and believe it is important not only to revive the celebration of their culture among themselves, but to share it with others. One of the practices that Aunty Mahealani teaches and does herself to get in the pono state of mind—clearing the negativity of the past and of modern life—is to start her day and greeting others with *"Aloha uhane,"* which is the acknowledgment of the connection to the soul or spirit. She says that many of her teachings come from her connection to the spirits of her ancestors, because they never died but have simply "changed address." As we waded in the hot pond and shared, I realized this was not a typical on-camera interview at all and that I was beginning to understand what the Hawaiians refer to as "talking story," the art of taking the time to share and to listen. Whether the people we met practiced the commonly known form of ho'oponopono or Aunty Mahealani's teaching of it, I learned that one of the keys to the healing power of ho'oponopono is the ability to share one's unique perception of an event, situation, or belief and then to have that perception completely seen and heard by others.

After meeting Aunty, my crew and I greeted each other every morning with "Aloha uhane" to remind us to live each day in pono. Plus, anyone who spends time traveling with me learns very quickly that I am not a morning person and need all the help I can get to feel positive at that time. Matt, whom I'd worked with on various shoots for over a decade, is one of the happiest people I've ever known any time of day, but particularly in the wee hours. He made it his mission to try to convince me of the wonders of getting up early.

"Ready for your morning serenade?" he asked as I lay there not yet ready to face our next shoot day. "Gah-fr-fr-num-num-num," I replied. Then, through the sheet I'd thrown over my head, the sweetest sounds filled my ears as Matt played a recording of the birdsong that he'd captured at first light.

One of Nancy's senior massage instructors, Paul Rambo, had arranged for us to visit one of the most beloved *kupuna* (elders) on the island, Uncle Robert. His full name, Robert Keliʻihoʻomalu (okay, the first step to mastering Hawaiian is to pronounce every syllable—come on, don't just skip over his name, try it—kay-lee-ee-ho-oh-ma-lu), means "prince of peace," and he is someone who is committed to living up to his name. An ambassador of Hawaiian culture, an activist in the Hawaiian sovereignty movement, and a community leader, Uncle Robert told us that his mission is to share.

Uncle Robert's place was in Kalapana, an area just east of Volcanoes National Park that was devastated by Pele's fury in 1990, with a magnificent black sand beach and most of the town buried by the Kilauea lava flow. He invited us to explore his Hawaiian Nature Walk and to learn of how he came to make this offering of his property as a place to teach about the Hawaiian way of life and the art of using medicinal plants, known as *lʻau lapaʻau.*

Meeting the prince of peace was like being in the presence of royalty—power blended with compassion and wisdom. Wearing a large wooden rosary and a ti leaf lei around his neck and looming over me at six-foot-four, this gentle giant put one hand on my shoulder and held the other one out for me to shake. We both giggled when we compared the size of our hands, his being nearly twice as large as mine. Uncle Robert was the embodiment of Aloha. His grand stature combined with a warm spirit made my crew and I feel instantly welcomed and cared for. One of the most important values to him, for which he credits the old Hawaiian way of life in which he was raised, is to take care of his *ohana* (family), not just his immediate family, but also his extended community—the greater ohana. Once invited to talk story with him, we were immediately adopted and embraced as part of his ever-expanding clan. As part of the ohana spirit, we were taught that whenever we are introduced to an elder, it is expected that they be addressed as Aunty or Uncle. The biggest challenge with that rule of etiquette is being able to assess correctly whether someone is older than you, lest you insult someone who is not.

We sat in the outdoor stand at the entrance of the Hawaiian Nature Walk as Uncle Robert told me what he calls his miracle story. In 1990 he was working for the county of Hawaii, and as Kilauea's massive flow approached his hometown, his job was to keep ahead of the fiery lava and put up barricades to keep people away from the danger zones and looters from entering homes that had been evacuated. Once the lava came around the bend and started to engulf what was once Kaimu black sand beach, he could see the lava approaching his home. His family was then evacuated up the hill, but his wife would come down to the edge of the flow every day, praying that the home where she raised eleven children with Uncle Robert would be spared.

As the flow seeped through the stone walls around his property, he begged his wife to leave, but she told him, "I raised eleven children here, and if it's going to go, at least I'm going to see it." As she stood her ground praying to God and beseeching Pele to have mercy, Uncle Robert says, "The flow came in front of her and stopped. And then started to build up, build up, build up. And, to her surprise, it started to reverse out to the road." He pointed to a spot just a few feet from where we were sitting and said, "From over there [it] came to my driveway ... and stopped right there, where the barricade is now. And from there it went to the ocean. All the time she was praying, crying, and I believe God performed a miracle. True story."

As an offering of thanksgiving, Uncle Robert and his family committed to opening up their property to others, creating the Hawaiian Nature Walk, and sharing their good fortune of having been able to live off the gifts of the land. Uncle Robert explained that there was another reason for the Nature Walk: "There's a lot of areas that have been cleaned and pushed, cleared away and destroyed all of this medicine that we used to have, and there's not too much now. So we have to contain all that we have and make it grow again. Bring it back." As we strolled through the Nature Walk's medicinal garden, he taught us about the various uses of the plants to heal, knowledge that was once handed down from generation to generation.

There were plants used to heal cuts, to eliminate thrush in babies, to cure ulcers, and to regulate diabetes. Uncle Robert even showed us a remedy for a lonely heart. "Sugar cane is our candy, but if you know how to prepare this, you can use it to make a love call. Give it to the woman, and the woman will fall in love with you. Oh, boy, I'll tell you. You'll pack your suitcase and all of you will follow me." He let out his mischievous giggle, looked over his shoulder, and skipped off to the next plant. Uncle Robert didn't need a love call to get me to follow him. His enthusiasm and delight for the plants and all they offered was irresistible. Uncle Robert also explained that there is a protocol when working with plant medicine. Rather than viewing the plant as an object for us to consume, it is to treat it with reverence for its gifts of healing. Before picking from a medicinal plant, Uncle Robert's mother taught him that first we must pray, think of the person for whom the medicine is being picked, and then have that person give thanks prior to receiving the remedy. I gave a lot of thanks when he rubbed the soothing juice of the *noni (Morinda citrifolia)* fruit on my mosquito bite–ridden skin to help reduce the itching and to keep the bites from getting infected.

We ended our tour with a tasting ceremony. Uncle Robert had us all hold hands and said a prayer, thanking God for the good company and the medicinal powers of what we were about to drink. First he gave each of us a cup of the noni juice, which he said was good for cleansing the system, but it felt better on my skin than it tasted on my tongue. Then we were treated to *awa (Piper methysticum)* tea, a brew that has been used in sacred ceremonies by many Polynesian cultures throughout history and that has a calming, relaxing effect. The noni tasted like what I imagined battery acid might be, and the awa was like chalk tea, but the Lucky Bastards and I felt honored to be sharing this experience with our generous host. Although several flows have affected Kalapana and its surrounding areas since 1990, Uncle Robert's property still stands and is now home to a farmers market,

Uncle Robert's Awa Bar, and Kalapana Cultural Tours, all run by his family and continuing to provide a happy gathering place for locals and tourists to share in the aloha spirit and the ohana experience.

After our time with Uncle Robert, Paul had a surprise for us. He wanted to take us to one of his secret hideaways. We pulled off along the side of the road outside the town of Pahoa. There were no signs or hints that there was anything special about the place we'd stopped. As we hiked through a forest of *ohiʻa (Metrosideros polymorpha)* trees, which were more like bushes, we saw mounds of rock sprouting out of the ground, completely hidden from the road by the brush. When we approached what Paul explained to be cinder cones, we could see that steam was wafting from deep cavities in their centers. Paul took us to the largest one, pointed to the gaping hole below us, and said, "After you." As we climbed down a ladder that he and his friends had put there some time ago, we saw a narrow crevice on one wall of the hole. When we slipped through it, we found ourselves in a cave that was big enough to house Paul and us four LBC members. Inside were two wooden planks, which we used as benches. Paul smiled and gave us instructions. "Welcome to Pele's natural sauna! Now, the temperature will vary in here, so if it suddenly gets really hot, don't panic. Just get up slowly and carefully step outside."

The natural saunas, or steam vents, are created when rainfall and groundwater seep into these pockets where lava once spewed and are heated by the geothermal energy of the nearby volcano. As we sat in the warmth of Pele's steam room, Paul shared that when he first visited Hawaii in the late seventies, after spending a month with the locals and being adopted by Uncle Robert, he was a changed man and knew he'd finally found a place where he felt he belonged. Paul then studied with many of the Hawaiian healers and elders to continue mastering the healing arts that he had begun to practice as a trained massage therapist and acupressure practitioner on the mainland. "From Uncle Robert, I learned that talking story is about having love in your heart and really listening, whether you're conversing with someone or it's the aina—the land or the elements—speaking to you," Paul explained. And from the lomilomi massage masters he studied intensively with, he learned that healing isn't just about doing something to someone to fix them; it's about being prayerful and bringing your best to the table as an offering. Paul closed his eyes and added, "The Hawaiians have an expression that describes oneness with God or spirit. Hawaii gives you the opportunity to dwell in that—not that I am God, but that I am a part of God, a part of spirit. It has that aroma, taste, and that aliveness you're looking for when you want to touch spirit."

As we sat there relaxing in the steam vent, being touched by the spirit of Pele's warmth and listening to Paul with love in our hearts, the temperature very suddenly spiked. Like most newbies who are trying to take in a lot of new information, I completely forgot about Paul's earlier instructions. Feeling like I was getting a karma hit for all those boiled-alive lobsters and crabs that I'd eaten throughout my life, I felt Pele's searing heat enveloping my body. I had a hard time breathing through the steam cloud that grew instantly thick. And yes, I panicked. I might even have shrieked. I shot straight up from the bench and dove toward the opening not even hesitating to see if my fellow spa pals were okay. The only thing that saved me from getting my head gashed open by the sharp rocks on the low ceiling was the fact that standing, I was just shy of the height of the cave. Years later, I would return to the steam vent with my then husband. This time I was cool, showing off a bit that I knew how to handle the heat. But the one thing I wasn't prepared for, looking out from the relaxing sauna, was seeing an old rat the size of a fat cat waddling around. As there was nowhere to run, I simply froze in the heat of the moment and hoped Pele would have mercy.

At the end of each day, after a stop at the farmers market, local store, or self-service produce stand lining the sides of the roads, where payment was done through the honor system, we'd reconvene at Nancy's home and prepare dinner together. Nancy generously opened her home to four strangers, made all the arrangements for interviews, helped us map out our shooting locations, and even gave us rides on her Harley. In exchange, we were in charge of making the meals. Because I'm abysmal in the kitchen, it was often Joseph, Matt, and Cora who handled the main courses, while I helped with side dishes and setting the table. Although Nancy was an accomplished international educator, entrepreneur (being the founder of two massage schools, a publishing company, and a healing retreat center), author, historian, and healer in her own right, she humbly deferred to the Hawaiian teachers in their presence. Trained in anatomy, sports medicine, reflexology, and various forms of massage, Nancy added to her knowledge base by studying and embracing Hawaiian culture and healing modalities after she married into a Hawaiian family and had her children. "When I set out to write the book on Hawaiian healing and lomilomi massage, I knew the first thing I needed to do was ask permission of the elders and teachers and get their blessing. Because there was such a strong loss of heritage when missionaries and colonization made practicing Hawaiian culture and speaking the native language a punishable crime, there was a time when the Hawaiians went underground with it, and to protect their precious traditions, had to make them kapu to be spoken of or shared," she explained. Nancy had to show the elders that her desire was to balance helping them to preserve and share the traditions while also respecting their need to protect what is theirs. As we talked story with Nancy and she prepared us for the next day's interviews, it was hard to imagine that we were ever anything but ohana as we shared meals and laughs, reviewed our footage, and put on slide shows of our daily adventures in paradise each evening.

Headed to Hilo, our next stop was to meet with our first lomilomi master, Aunty Mary Fragas. Although there is no universal lomilomi technique, as the practice can vary from lineage to lineage, there are some commonalities among the various practices, such as using the forearms more than the hands to knead the body, doing deep tissue work to "cleanse the bones," or using certain rhythmic patterns of motion. Nancy explained that what makes lomilomi most distinctive, however, is this: "It's all the benefits of massage therapy combined with unconditional love. It's a loving touch and is prayerful work. When you combine that with all the soft tissue work, it enables you to release all the stress and experience a higher level of being."

When we entered Aunty Mary's healing room, she greeted us with a generous smile, gentle eyes peering from behind large glasses, and a melodious "Aloha!" She was seated on the floor next to a mat where her patients would receive her treatments. Because she had survived childhood polio, it was difficult for her to walk long distances or to stand, so she did all her work on the floor. When she was diagnosed at the age of six with the disease, which affects nerve cells in the brain stem and spinal cord, the doctors at the hospital had condemned her to death and refused to give her treatment. Aunty Mary explained, "Every day I kept crying and said, 'Mommy, I don't want to die!' Mamma'd get mad at me and would say, 'You're not gonna die!' And for sure, I'm not going to die. I'm seventy-six! You know, I think all those doctors have died." We both laughed. Her mother rejected the doctors' prognosis and brought Aunty Mary back to her family for Hawaiian traditional healing—exercises, herbal medicine, and lomilomi massage. Aunty Mary added, "Because of that, as I grew up ... in my mind, I must help people."

Aunty Mary was known for her ability to diagnose accurately through palpation and intuition and then to be able to make physical corrections. One of her specialties was prenatal massage, or using lomilomi to help alleviate symptoms of difficult pregnancies. But she explained that she could treat anything from headaches to backaches, bone fractures to asthma. Aunty Mary added that most people came to her after they'd tried many other treatments without relief from their symptoms, which were usually due to old injuries. She shared a story in which a man had suffered from chronic headaches all his life. When she'd intuited that it went back to his time in utero, he thought she was nuts. So Aunty Mary advised him to ask his mother if she'd had a fall while she was pregnant with him and if she, too, had chronic headaches. As it turned out, the man's mother had indeed fallen two stories while she was pregnant with him and had had constant headaches since then. After that, the man was sold, and it was decided that Aunty Mary would treat both mother and son.

We felt the best way for me to understand lomilomi was to experience it firsthand, so I volunteered to lay down on her floor and let her go to town. I was on my stomach, and immediately upon laying her hands on me—one on my shoulder and one on my hip—Aunty Mary exclaimed, "Oh, wow! You were in an impact. In other words, you were in a fall."

She then touched my upper back and added, "This is not normal. This hump here shows that there was an accident." She was able to determine that I'd fallen on my tailbone at some point and had caused compression in my spine, which was true; I had done that in a dirt-bike accident. She continued her diagnosis: "Problems like this would always cause a low back pain. Is that what you go through?" "Uh huh," I replied. "Mm hmm. And if there's low back pain, that means there's pain in the neck, too. Right in the nape here," she said as she massaged my low back and neck. As she continued to massage my body, she was able to diagnose accurately that I also had a history of anemia, asthma, and feeling cold at night.

What struck me the most about Aunty Mary, besides her keen ability to diagnose and her delight as she worked, was the power of her hands. It seemed that all she'd lost to polio in the use of her legs, God gave back to her in the use of her arms and hands. When she pushed them down on my forehead, what she called "smashing the brain," it felt like my head was being crushed, yet somehow it felt good, as if all the mental rubbish was being squished out of it. Just as those hands were strong enough to move muscle, tendons, and joints, they were also gently warm and soothing when she put them over my eyes, explaining, "This is feeding the eyeballs." When she found the scar from my ACL repair on my left knee, I explained that I'd torn the ligament when I hit a tree on a sled. She replied, "Oh, that's a mean one. You hit a tree? And, it didn't move for you?" She let out her Yoda-like laugh. Then she grabbed both my arms, put them above my head, and pulled several times. I was getting stretched and rocked at the same time. That would be a recurring feeling as I continued on my journey meeting healers—being expanded and having my world rocked to the core.

When Aunty Mary was done with me, I got up and actually felt as if I were off-kilter. "Yes, because you were used to leaning wrong for so long," Aunty explained. Before leaving, I thanked her for the treatment and for sharing her story with us. "Don't mention. I'm glad you came," she said, and as we hugged, she got one last bit of healing in by drumming up and down my back with her cupped hands. I'd asked Aunty Mary if she had a name for what she does, and she replied, "Not really. Just that I care."

Just as Aunty Mary kneaded, tugged, and loved away all the places where I was holding—peeling away all my protective compensating patterns—crossing the threshold from director to subject stripped away a shield I didn't even know I had been hiding behind. Having my frailties and wounds diagnosed, treated, and documented on camera left me feeling emotional, wobbly, and exposed. Luckily, the only thing Cora had planned for us that afternoon was to get some beauty shots, which would not require too much thinking on my part. I also knew I could count on Joseph's cinematography genius to capture the essence of the raw natural splendor that surrounded us.

We visited Wailuku River State Park just outside of Hilo, home of the longest river in the Hawaiian Islands, snaking through eighteen miles of lush terrain and encompassing the eighty-foot-tall Rainbow Falls and the terraced pools known as Boiling Pots. Rainbow Falls was easily accessible, and we took our time making our way behind the cascade, taking in the rainbows that appeared when the sunlight hit the spray. About two miles upstream, we explored Boiling Pots and were mesmerized by the churning pools. Sensing my vulnerability, Cora, Joseph, and Matt left me to collect myself while they hiked down to continue shooting—Cora with her still camera, Joseph pushing our small video camera to its maximum capabilities, and Matt capturing the song of gurgling water.

As I watched them climbing rocks and wading in the river, I began to realize that my discomfort at feeling defenseless was giving way to a sense of lightness of being. Somehow without all the layers it seemed I could hear the water, the wind, and the birds more clearly. I was experiencing what I would later learn from my teachers—that a heart newly opened first feels all the pain it has been trying to protect itself from, but if it is patient and continues to unfurl, it soon discovers that behind the veil is a vast expanse. Sitting on a ledge peering down at the pools and my fellow LBC adventurers, the rawness that previously caused me to want to recoil transformed into a powerful sensation I could only liken to being in love—not with any particular person or object of desire, but with everything that lay before me. I began to have a visceral experience of living aloha.

On our last day in Hawaii, I was awakened not by birdsong but by a ukulele. The tune sounded familiar as the music came closer and closer. I opened my eyes to find Matt, strumming the instrument and grinning. In response to my vehement protests of "Go away," he broke out in an improv version of The Kingsmen's "Louie Louie."

> *Marie-Rose, Oh Oh*
> *She got no pono*
> *No no no no no*
> *Been three days and three nights in Hilo*
> *And still she ain't got no pono*
> *No no no no no*
> *And we gotta go now*

I really did need to get my pono on and get out the door that morning because we were invited to shoot a rare event—a sacred ceremony and a lomilomi massage at Volcanoes National Park. Papa Sylvester Kepelino, or Papa K, as he was affectionately called, was one of the few elders who had special permission to perform rituals and healing work within the park on what the Hawaiians consider to be holy ground. Nancy told us that Papa K was granted this rare honor not only because he was a master of lomilomi but also because he was considered a *kahuna* (priest, healer, expert) by his Hawaiian community. To receive the title of kahuna, one has to have trained in the traditional Hawaiian spiritual and healing arts with a recognized kahuna, and be able to trace back the lineage of the teachings.

Papa K was chosen to carry on his family's tradition at the age of six by his grandfather, an established kahuna, and then received further training from his father. Papa K would tell me, "In the old days, if you were chosen, you had to study for years and years and go through a lot of processing. You learned about physical medicine, herbal medicine, and spiritual medicine." At the age of eight, after having received some lessons on living off the land and using medicinal herbs, Papa K was taken to a remote area on the island and left there for twenty-one days to fend for himself. The terrors that filled little Sylvester's days and nights in the Hawaiian wilderness were physical, such as thirst, hunger, cold, and aggressive wild boars, and psychospiritual, as every night he heard spirits calling his name and speaking to him. This initiation was not just about surviving the elements, but also a test of his spiritual fortitude and faith. After the three weeks were over, his grandfather snuck up behind him, picked him up, and laughingly told him the test was over. The startled child at first kicked and hit his elder out of shock and fear, then cried tears of relief and joy. That day, he'd passed his initiation and was on his way to becoming a powerful healer.

When Nancy first introduced us to Papa K in Volcanoes National Park, he was friendly and jovial in his dress shorts, Hawaiian print shirt, and huge straw hat. She told us that after his intense training as a kahuna, he'd gone to the mainland to pursue some of his other passions. He worked as a chef and entertainer in Las Vegas, and his onstage persona and flare for presentation were evident as he joked with the men and flirted with the women in our group. On the surface, his other pursuits could not have been more divergent from his upbringing. But during his time in Sin City, Papa K was exposed to a bigger world, and he felt it gave him a greater perspective on ancient healing's place in modern life. Papa K returned to Hawaii years later with a calling to share his knowledge to as many people as possible. As he changed out of his resort wear and into a more traditional outfit—a crimson red cloth garment wrapped around his body and tied around his neck, with a boar-tusk necklace. The affable fellow had transformed into a kahuna with a commanding presence.

Nancy and his assistant, Kathleen, both longtime students of Papa K's and part of his ohana, helped him to set up the healing area per his instructions. They placed the massage table on flat ground among trees, at the precise spot he'd chosen near one of the volcanic craters. The women then cut through some ti leaves to create fringes and attached them along the edges of the table and to each leg for decorative and protective purposes. As he prepared and blessed the elements from the island, such as saltwater, volcanic rocks, and wooden bowls, Papa K explained these were all sacred and held the healing energy of this powerful place. And although there were techniques, training, and tools to be used during lomilomi, the most important element to him was that of *pule,* prayer. Papa K explained, "The prayers are the first things we learn before attempting to even work on a person's body. In these prayers I'll pray to our Father Almighty for healing of the person that I work on." The Hawaiian prayers that Papa K knew, which were passed down from generation to generation, were so sacred that he realized he needed to preserve them. Over time, Papa K had written them all down and translated them, giving copies to Paul for safekeeping should anything ever happen to him.

Papa K instructed Nancy, Kathleen, and our team to gather in a circle around the massage table with him. We joined hands while he spoke a Hawaiian prayer, which sounded more like a chant. Afterward, Kathleen climbed on the table so Papa K could demonstrate how he worked or, as he put it, how the work moved through him. "There's only two things I ask of a patient when I work with them," he said. "The first thing is faith and the second is trust. The reason I say faith and trust is because I'm not actually the complete healer. I just do the work. Because the person I believe in that I work with is God. He's the actual healer and I am his vehicle. He drives my hands, tells me where to go to work on a person who's hurting. Shows me what to do and tells me how to do it."

Because healing for Papa K was not just a physical endeavor, but also an energetic transfer, he began every session by rubbing saltwater on the patient to help cleanse them and to prevent any illnesses from being transferred to him, and then followed that with rubbing oil in the areas where he'd be working. He explained that his hands not only transmitted healing energy, but also received information. After he'd worked along Kathleen's spine, around her shoulders, and down her arms and legs, he rested his hand on her calf and said that through his fingers, "I can feel the person's pain ... I can say, 'oh, your back hurts, or your feet hurt, or your shoulders hurt, or your tummy hurts' ... see, with my fingers ... I can feel where the pain is because actually ... it feels like needles poking my hand ... my palm can get so hot. I just lay it on the spot and bring it [the pain] up to the surface." He ended her healing with, "This is what we call Hawaiian lomilomi, and it is very gentle and loving touch."

Seeing the love with which Papa K did the work was so moving that I actually found myself in tears. He noticed me behind the camera trying to hide my emotions and came over to me. When Papa K wrapped his arms around me, stroked the back of my head, and began to say a Hawaiian prayer, there was no way I could contain myself. The waterworks were unstoppable. Upon finishing the prayer, he blessed me from top to bottom and then whispered its meaning in my ear. "*Ikaika* means to be strong. Be strong in the Lord and he will help you anytime you feel sad. Talk to him. Ask for love. Ask for guidance. He is always there for you and I promise you, you will always be safe in his arms, his blessings. Amen." He then kissed each of my eyes, wiped the tears from my cheeks, and continued, "They must be tears of joy, not tears of sadness." He then pointed to my heart followed by my head and said, "It's your heart that's important ... your thoughts are important." He put his hands on my shoulders and closed with, "A kahuna has told you and he loves you, so always be happy." It seemed Papa K took over where Aunty Mary had left off with breaking down my defenses and keeping me connected to my heart and emotions.

I had some time to collect myself as we traveled to another location where Papa K would make an offering to the goddess Pele to thank her for the use of her land for healing. We ended up in an area of the park where the steam vents were plentiful and thick white plumes filled the air, giving the ritual a greater feeling of the mystical. Papa K held a bundle wrapped in ti leaves, a *ho'okupu* (ceremonial gift), over a crevasse with steam flowing from it, and began to chant to the goddess he refers to as *tutu* (grandmother) Pele, a familiar term that only someone confident in his intimate connection with her would dare use. As he chanted, I felt transported to a place where goddesses do hear our prayers, the universe is on our side, and we are meant to be happy.

After the ceremony, Papa K came over to me and said, "I'd like to send two of my owls with you. We call them *pueos,* my messengers. They'll be guiding your path wherever you go. And if anything's wrong, they'll let me know." I thanked him and he gave me one last hug, put his straw hat on, and walked away. As he did, a heavy rain came down on us. Paul would later tell me that part of Papa K's kahuna magic was to be able to affect the weather. He'd said, "Didn't you notice that the whole time we were at Volcanoes it was threatening to rain, but it stayed away until after

Papa K was done with the ceremony and you guys were done shooting?"
I could not deny it.

Before leaving paradise, we got in a plane and flew over the volcano to get some footage of the lava flow. I was mesmerized as I watched the hot flow meet the cool sea. Just as Pele destroys what lies in her path, she is also giving birth to new land and expanding her boundaries. I found the Big Island to be a place where we have the opportunity to bridge apparent dualities, where the mystical can be touched, and where the pain of growth is equal to the joy of discovery. As the searing lava rolled over the land, I realized hot tears were streaming down my cheeks. They were tears of gratitude for all that I had been given here, and tears of sadness at having to leave.

> "God turns you from one feeling to another and teaches by means
> of opposites so that you will have two wings to fly, not one."
>
> —Mawlana Jalaluddin Rumi, *Rumi Daylight*

CHAPTER 5

Initiation Part 2

Back to Peru (Crossing the Threshold, Part 2)

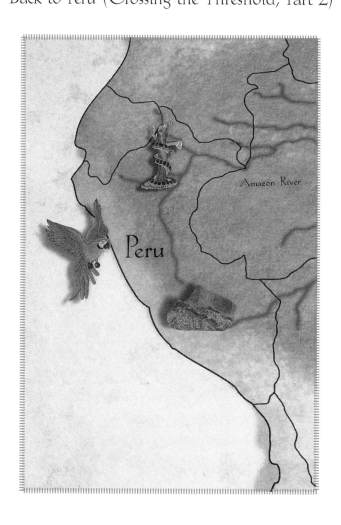

We'd all been prepped to understand that the taking of aya-huasca, a complex brew of psychoactive plants, was not a recreational activity but rather a sacred rite. Some of us felt honored to accept the invitation of a local shaman to participate in his ceremony, while some would only attend as witnesses. We'd all agreed that whatever happened in the shack along the banks of the Ucayali River, it would remain a private, personal endeavor that we were embarking on together, and not meant to be put on-camera. Some of us were terrified, some of us were excited, but none of us knew what to expect as the sha-man poured from a bright yellow Pennzoil jug the appropriate dose of ayahuasca for each individual. The shaman and his wife would be there to attend to our needs and to keep us tethered to a safe place as we traveled. They told us we would meet the darkest of our fears and the brightest of our soul's potential. They cautioned us to be on the lookout for beings from both camps—demons and angels—who would appear to pull us to the light or to the darkness. But, all would be potential teachers to help us face what we needed to heal within ourselves and to give us instructions on our soul's path.

The shaman and his wife had warned us that we would feel nauseous and that it would be best if we didn't fight, but rather just gave in to the urge to vomit. The more we allowed our stomachs to be cleansed, the more powerful the effects would be. Even though they had provided us with mats to lie on and buckets to purge into, I stubbornly insisted on going to the bathroom to let the concoction do its work. When I stood up, I didn't expect to already feel the dizziness and the distortion of my senses as I stumbled to the area where there was a hole cut out of the floor that opened to a marshy pit below. As my system let go of everything it no longer needed, I prayed that I wouldn't tumble with it into the darkness.

Less than two months after lamenting having to leave paradise, the LBC reunited to join me on my return trip to Peru. Lisa, the CEO of the California-based natural pharmaceutical company, had commissioned us to document a rain forest walk with Pablo and to create a video to educate her potential investors on the viability of pharmaceuticals derived from the rain forest. Because I had done my location scout just a few months prior, Cora and I were able to plan this trip easily. Matt and Joseph were eager to have another adventure and relished the opportunity to brush up on their Spanish. It turned out that Joseph had lived in Mexico for a few years after college, so was nearly fluent, which would come in handy during our interviews. Matt took three years of classes in high school and then picked up some basic conversational skills on his travels working for National Geographic and Discovery Channel, which would make for some creative conversations during our shoot. Once we landed in Lima and the Spanish started to flow, our boys transformed into Mateo and Pepe, and strutted off the plane ready to show their stuff.

It was great to see Carina and Elsa again, who were there to greet us at our hotel in Lima. The three of us hoped the lessons learned from our scout would allow us to have smoother sailing for the shoot. Once again, it was a short night in Lima followed by a quick flight the next morning to Pucallpa. This time, our travels getting there were purposefully uneventful, with all of us being mindful to keep our bags close to us and Elsa having arranged for us to cab directly to the hotel in Pucallpa, rather than have anyone meet us. We were well out of mud season, so we had no issues getting there. Arriving at the same hotel on the edge of the *selva* (jungle), I experienced it anew through the eyes of Cora, Mateo, and Pepe. What I appreciated most about my fellow Lucky Bastards was that they delighted in the simplest of things, which made even the mundane seem special. Whether we were drinking coca tea with breakfast pastries, sharing meals of roast chicken with plantains and yucca, or diving into the alga-laden hotel pool, everything was treated like an exotic escapade.

Years later, Mateo would tell me, "One of my most vivid life memories takes me back to our times in Pucallpa, Peru—staying at the odd little hotel, which probably had a fair amount of drug running keeping it in business—when the laundry lady outside our rooms started cranking Bon Jovi ... pure cognitive dissonance." We agreed the song she was blaring that day was "Livin' on a Prayer."

In the morning, we all headed to the Usko Ayar School of Painting to make plans with Don (a title of respect) Pablo and some of his former students, who like Wellington were now volunteer teachers and organizers. Some had started their own studios, some helped at Usko Ayar in Pucallpa, and others worked in the outreach program, traveling along the Ucayali River to teach village children in their own environments. When I arrived with the crew, Don Pablo was playing the guitar, tapping his foot to create a rhythmic accompaniment while his brother sang. It was a great way to set the tone for our time together and for the gang to be introduced to a unique shaman. Having had the awe-inspiring experience of the rain forest's grandeur from atop its canopy, I was now looking forward to digging deeper than its beauty by learning about its medicinal value and spiritual secrets from Don Pablo.

We all jumped in the peke peke, which just happened to be aptly named *Pablito's* (Little Pablo's) *Tours,* and journeyed downriver. I asked our boat driver why the water taxis were called peke peke, and he smiled and said, "Because it's the noise the engine and propeller make: peke peke peke peke." When we arrived at the little village, Wellington rang the school bell, and children came scurrying from all directions. The schoolhouse was a small thatched hut, elevated about five feet off the ground to accommodate the rising of the river during flood season. I'd never seen children so happy to be in school. The group of six- to ten-year-olds sat on the floor and listened as Don Pablo told them what they would be working on that day. After the school supplies were handed out, the children formed a circle, lay on the floor, and then began to draw, while Don Pablo and his assistants walked around giving instruction and encouragement. Most people who visit remote villages in developing countries tend to bring candy for the children, but we learned that this causes too many dental and health problems. School supplies, toys, and toothbrushes were better alternatives. Cora, who had traveled extensively, had prepared us by loading up on pencils, sharpeners, erasers, and paper prior to our departure from Seattle.

Don Pablo explained to us that art was "a vehicle for giving my students integral education. They learn to respect, to love the humankind, the animals, the plants, and the rain forest," which would lead to them learning to love themselves. Elsa, who is of Andean descent and suffered her fair share of discrimination, added, "It's important for the kids to realize that there isn't such a thing as a superior or inferior culture. To educate oneself on how to survive in one's own environment in a sustainable manner is the most important thing."

After the classwork was complete, it was time for the lab portion. We gathered all the kids into the peke peke and continued upriver to a spot where we would take a rain forest walk. Just as I was getting off the boat, I stopped in my tracks when I saw at the water's edge what looked like a rat as big as a medium-size dog. The children laughed when they noticed I was frozen with fear, while they just shrugged it off and walked right by the thing. I had read about capybaras, the largest rodents in the world, who in truth are much cuter than rats, but seeing it in actuality was a bit intimidating. Wellington held out his hand for me; I grabbed it, jumped off the boat, and made a run for the forest.

Why was I shouting? When I used to look at photos of the rain forest, it never occurred to me that it would be a noisy place. It took some getting used to how loud it actually was. As we walked through the underbrush, we found ourselves raising our voices in order to hear each other over the cacophony of sounds—the high-pitched whistling of monkeys, the croaking of frogs, the songs of birds, the chirps of insects. It was indicative of how teeming with life the rain forest was. Engulfed by its lushness, it was hard to imagine the fragility of the rain forest's existence, with its destruction by those needing farmland or firewood to survive, and by those hungry for the riches its natural resources command on the global market.

Walking among the wildlife in the rain forest was bittersweet for Don Pablo, who delighted in its wonders yet was acutely aware of its existence slipping away with each passing day. His hope was that the knowledge and memory of its wisdom and mysteries would be carried forth by the children and that the awareness of its importance would be spread through his art. "The forest is a silent factory that produces oxygen and food for everyone on the planet and needs to be taken care of," he told the kids. As we moved through the bushes and giant trees, Don Pablo would stop by various plants giving lessons on their healing properties and then sprinkling the teachings with opportunities for play. This was an interactive school at its best, with the children touching, smelling, and tasting some of the plants, and then laughing and screaming as they swung from vines, jumped over rocks, and climbed trees.

Strolling through the rain forest with Don Pablo was like combing through the aisles of nature's drugstore. "This plant is called *caña agria* or *sacha auiro*. This is a medicinal plant and is really good for treating bronchitis," Don Pablo said, reaching for an elongated leaf of a bushy plant. We approached a tree that was about eighty feet tall and as he pointed our gaze up the length of its trunk, Don Pablo added, "The bark of this tree is good for treating arthritis and internal bleeding." Further along our walk, Wellington demonstrated how to dig up roots of the plant that helped to cure his malaria and said he'd teach us how to make a tea decoction to take with us should we need it during our time in the rain forest. Mateo showed Don Pablo his puffy elbow, which had been inflamed for weeks, perhaps due to a hazard of his occupation: having to hold a boom mic pole over his head for hours a day. Don Pablo walked up to a young tree, cut into the bark, and collected the milky sap. He gently rubbed the sticky stuff into Mateo's elbow and explained that it was a powerful anti-inflammatory. Most people are not aware that many of the medicines used in operating rooms today are derived from plants that have been traditionally used by indigenous peoples of the Amazon for centuries.

Like most shamans, Don Pablo will tell you that he learned about plant medicine from his teachers and from the spirits of the rain forest, who tell the shamans which plants to use for what ailments and give instructions on the proper administration of the medicine. Many ethnobotanists admit that they are baffled and amazed by the chemical complexity and accuracy of the shamans' medicines and their efficacy in treating various illnesses.

"The planet is full of spirits in the plants, in the river, into the earth," Don Pablo said passionately, waving his hands in the air and then pointing his fingers downward. He added that although we may not be able to see them with the naked eye, they are all around us. When I asked if he could see the spirits, Don Pablo replied, "Yes, sometimes I can see them when I'm concentrating, because I am like a priest. When I was a shaman, I was in close contact with them."

At the last village we visited, the children treated us to a dance performance. They danced holding hands, moving around in a circle, and passing through a hula hoop–like ring. I was told this was a dance celebrating the circle of life. As I watched them smiling and moving gracefully, never breaking their connection to one another, I thought of Don Pablo's words: "Children are like plants. In order to grow, they must be cared for, and like the plants and the forest, they are our future."

After we returned to Uska Ayar a few days later, Don Pablo and his former students were teaching a group of children to paint what they experienced in the rain forest. The children learned to paint trees, rivers, skies, and animals. Don Pablo closed the class with, "Artistry is found in one's heart and mind. Painters that have both—skill and imagination—are true artists." Watching Don Pablo leading the children in the classroom and in the rain forest, I understood that he was not only bridging the material and spiritual worlds, but also bridging the old world of shamanism and the modern world that was creeping in. He was a man whose culture was in transition and who'd made a conscious choice to help the next generation move with that change, rather than deny or resist it.

We ended our time with Don Pablo, Wellington, and the rest of his Usko Ayar gang with a celebration dinner out. Mateo decided he'd like to order the appetizers for the table. When he proudly ordered in Spanish, meaning to ask for *anticuchos* (skewered meat) there was a moment of dead silence and then an explosion of laughter all around us. Apparently, rather than asking for the appetizers, he'd somehow inadvertently ordered anti-penises.

We didn't find the *ayahuascero* (ayahuasca shaman); his wife had approached Elsa, letting her know of the opportunity by the edge of the river. In the years since our visit to the Amazon, ayahuasca ceremonies have become popular tourist attractions. With the promise of easy money from naive spiritual or thrill seekers, many sham shamans have cropped up who have neither the spiritual training nor the integrity to make the brew as medicine or to lead the ceremony for healing. There have been reports of unfortunate participants experiencing sexual abuse, psychological damage, and even death from the inappropriate actions of these con men. We were lucky. Because Elsa was *peruana* (Peruvian) and had spent most of her adult life among indigenous people doing ethnobotanical research, she was "jungle savvy" and was extremely protective of her LBC wards. Because she'd checked with her sources and vetted the shaman and his wife, we knew we were getting the real deal. Equally important to Elsa as the shaman's authenticity was our earnest desire to respect, understand, and experience a traditional Amazonian custom and spiritual pathway. None of us were in it to just get high or go trippin'. In fact, we were warned that far from being a joyride, the experience is physically, emotionally, and spiritually demanding. This journey was not about escaping, but rather facing oneself.

If we would have had the time to prepare, for two weeks prior to taking ayahuasca we would have been on a cleansing diet of plain foods, maybe rice and boiled fish, with no meats, no sugar, no spices, no alcohol, no dairy. It would have also been a time to contemplate our commitment to our spiritual evolution and our opening to the spirit of ayahuasca, the vine of the soul. But, as it was, we had a couple of hours to rest and then walk along dirt roads to the shaman's ceremonial hut.

We were told to set an intention or to pose a question to the spirits before taking the medicine. I don't know that I really had a chance to taste the brew before I experienced my body's repulsion to it and my desire to hurl. Despite the shaman's instructions not to fight the urge, I really thought I could get away with not throwing up. I couldn't. After a few minutes of pointless struggle and bravado, it was time to surrender. When most of us had purged, the shaman began to sing the icaros, his sacred song to carry us into the other realms. It wasn't until I felt his voice lifting me up from the ground that I realized the journey had begun. The hallucinogenic effects of the medicine had kicked in.

The first thing I noticed was that it felt as if a protective layer over my senses was removed so that any sights, sounds, and sensations were acutely perceived—the rustling of my neighbor's fingertips moving over her cloth mat, a cockroach's footsteps as it approached my face, the vibrant colors of the new world that was coming into focus. There was an underlying sense of anxiety as I tried to navigate through this new reality, where movement was initiated through thought. I discovered that if I didn't like where I was, I could think myself to another scene if I concentrated.

Like many people traveling on ayahuasca's wings, I saw a serpent that spoke to me—not with its mouth, but in my head. It then became opaque and its skin formed a veil over everything. The skin moved and created rainbow colors just as fish scales might do when catching the light at different angles. It took me a while to realize I could speak in this realm. So, I asked a question: "Why is there a snakeskin over everything?" The serpent's telepathic response was, "Because we are all joined by a sacred membrane that connects all things. Separation is an illusion." At one point, when I was in a dark place with the terrorizing experience of being trapped in my dead body, I began to panic. Almost immediately, I felt a gentle caress on my skin, which turned out to be the shaman's wife blowing smoke over me, but it felt as if she were actually touching me. As the smoke surrounded me, it felt like she was embracing me. Simultaneously, I also heard a high-pitched call of the shaman. Although he was singing, his voice created a sound like none I had ever heard. It was as if he were singing and whistling at the same time. I remember thinking, "This must be what angels sound like." It was a clear comforting beacon calling me home, back to the hut until I felt safe again to travel. I then saw my own resurrection, as I rose out of a crypt from a mummified state into the land of the living. I was later told that it was the shaman's job to know where each of his patients was traveling and to stand at the ready to bring them back whenever they get lost.

When I looked over at Mateo, I saw him smiling and reaching his hands in the air, as if he were catching fireflies. He later reported that he'd actually been able to see and touch sound. He also heard the croaking of the frogs and chirping of insects as a choir. Some of the other travelers would become fearful, and I would think to them, "Don't worry. The shaman and his wife will bring you back," as if they could hear me. When I reached out to comfort a neighbor, my touch on her skin was so abrasive she freaked out and slapped my hand away. Once again, the shaman's wife came to the rescue, brushing her lightly with smoke. If I had known what I know now about the hypersensitivity of the senses, I would never have touched or spoken to anyone during the ceremony.

As the light of dawn began to creep into the hut, I was given one more message. The spirits showed me an image of a fierce warrior woman. In my egoic mind, I thought, "Yeah—that's me!" A voice quickly came in and chided me, saying, "If you meet the world with your sword drawn, you will only attract to yourself conflict. If, however, you keep it in its sheath on your belt, you will find you rarely have to use it. This is the power of the divine feminine."

Seven years after I had my first ayahuasca experience, I met a musician who'd formerly been in a Seattle grunge band and traveled the world to study ethnomusicology. He'd given me a recording he'd made of the icaros of the Shipibo people. It turned out he had visited the same villages I had, so the icaros were the same as the ones that ushered me into the other worlds. Whenever I listen to that music, I begin to get that floaty feeling again—my spirit separating from my body—and I know I should not operate heavy machinery, drive, or do anything but lie down and let it carry me back to those realms, or turn it off quickly and stay in the world I've chosen to inhabit. The feeling of being tethered by the shaman and his wife also stays with me after all this time. Whenever I feel overwhelmed or challenged by my life's situations, I have a visceral memory of being caressed, sung to, and held. I am reminded that there is no separation, and I feel safe.

CHAPTER 6

Mindfold

Kathmandu, Nepal (Tests, Allies, Enemies)

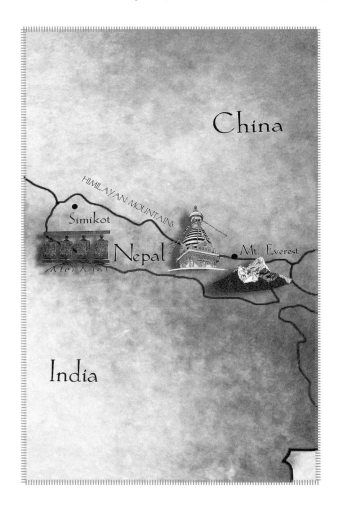

Joseph travels with a sleeping mask called Mindfold. It is designed to shut out the light and keep you in total darkness, even with your eyes open, to aid with sleeping and dreaming. Mindfold is the best way to describe our experiences in Nepal—a shutting out of routine thinking; a displacement of ordinary reality so that the extraordinary can be perceived; a state where all reference points have been redrawn—mind bending over on itself.

Since my return from that odyssey, I have spent these past fourteen years vacillating between working to get my mind back to where it was before I embarked on the journey and grasping the meaning of the creases Nepal left behind. Perhaps some things are not meant to be immediately understood. Perhaps when experiences are too dense for the psyche to process, they need to stew awhile until they are broken down into bite-size digestible morsels.

After thirty-six hours of travel and crossing several time zones, we landed in Kathmandu, the starting place of our quest to seek out some of the healers of Nepal.

Despite the jet lag, I felt surprisingly well—centered, grounded, not excited, but "insighted" with a feeling that all was right. There is a thirteen-hour and forty-five-minute time difference between Nepal and Seattle. Nepal is one of two places whose time is always fifteen minutes off from the rest of the world. It seems a place moving to its own rhythm.

For this leg of the journey, Cora had done an amazing job of getting us here with only four weeks of prep time. She, Joseph, and I were joined by Karel, a strong director of photography in his own right, who agreed to shoot second camera and take over sound duties, since Matt had to stay home to tend to family matters. We were met at Tribhuvan Airport by our local producer and guide, Thomas Kelly, a photo activist who had lived in the Himalayas for over two decades. It was at Thomas's invitation that we were in Nepal. He had access to the sacred sites in and around Kathmandu, and was a gatekeeper to many of the shamans and healers in this part of Asia. Thomas's personal interest in healing and spirituality had led him to sittings with *saddhus* (Hindu holy men), rituals with *lamas* (Tibetan Buddhist monks), and sacred pilgrimages with dhamis (Nepali shamans). In addition, he'd roamed the world to shed light on human rights issues such as the challenges facing indigenous cultures, the effects of wars on women and children, and the proliferation of human sex-slave trafficking.

When Thomas rattled off his itinerary for us, this lanky, six-foot-one, blond-haired, blue-eyed American man spoke with an accent and timbre shaped by years of the Nepali language rolling off his tongue. Having no experience in this part of the world, we had to put all our trust in his expertise. Thomas had scheduled what he called "two light shoot days" in Kathmandu, which would be followed by a weeklong trek to Humla, a remote area in the northwest corner of Nepal that borders Tibet. Day 1 would consist of shooting at a nearby Buddhist monastery at 5 a.m., moving to the sacred Boudhanath Stupa, visiting a Himalayan herb company, and purchasing gifts for those we would be visiting. Day 2 would entail touring the holy Hindu site of Pashupatinath and picking up the last of our trekking supplies prior to catching an afternoon flight to Nepalgung, the jumping-off point for our later flight to Simikot, Humla. I wondered what his idea of a heavy day would be.

We were lucky to be staying at Happy Valley Guesthouse in the Boudha area of town. This guesthouse boasted the rare amenities in Kathmandu of large clean rooms, private showers, and glorious views of the Great Stupa of Boudhanath—a sacred place of worship. Before first light, we were greeted by the sounds of devotion—chanting, drumming, and the *radong* (telescopic horn) calling all to prayer. During breakfast on the terrace, we witnessed the stream of worshipers below, circumambulating the 118-foot-tall domed stupa (domed Buddhist shrine) and growing from a devout few to a massive crowd all moving in an uninterrupted flow.

Draped with long streams of colorful prayer flags, the stupa's tower was adorned with the Buddha's eyes of equanimity painted on each of its walls, looking out in the four directions, and when seen from above, the stupa and its surrounding grounds form a sacred mandala.

Spiritual practice and celebration of multiple faiths were evident as Hindus, Buddhists, and others worshiped alongside one another. Despite the poverty and challenges of survival, these devotees rise early each day with the diligence of faith. When I later walked along the edge of the stupa, I was moved by the inertia of all those who circumambulate this sacred place with fierce intention to pray and offer this practice not only for themselves but for the sake of all sentient beings. It was comforting to think that my prayers and steps around the stupa that day could ripple out to help others and that after I left, there would be a continuous stream of people praying for my sake and that of so many others.

I could not get that Bob Seger song "Katmandu" out of my head. I blame this on missing our friend and sound guy, Matt. During the planning of this shoot back home, he'd felt compelled to do his best rendition of the classic rock icon, singing his ode to "dropping out" every time I mentioned the city. Although Matt wasn't here, his mischievous spirit was lurking. So, as Thomas led us on our whirlwind tour from the Shechen monastery to the sacred stupa, to the tourist haven of Thamel, past rock walls and dusty roads teeming with people, cars, mopeds, wandering dogs, and the occasional still cow, Matt was with us, belting out the score to our travels: "K-K-K-K-K-K-Katmandu."

By the time we met Tenzin Norbu of Sunny Travel trekking company, at his Himalayan Herb factory, we'd already been shooting for seven hours. Tenzin was born in Humla, and was encouraged to create both these enterprises in Kathmandu—a tour guide service and the manufacture of herbal products—by Thomas and his wife, anthropologist Carroll Dunham, to provide a means of economic sustainability for Humlis (people from the Humla villages) and to introduce visitors to Humla's unique cultures. Tenzin not only organized our trek but also took time from his constantly ringing cell phone (a sign of his success) to make himself available to educate us on the background and customs of the people of his home villages.

Tenzin explained that once we got to Humla, we would be spending most of our time in the Nyinba (Sunny Valley) villages of Baraunse, Torpa, Limitang, and Bargaun. "We are Nepali, but our ancestors migrated from western Tibet in search of hidden paradises, or Shangri-la, so we see ourselves as more like Tibetans," Tenzin said. Thomas added that the Nyinbas (people of the Sunny Valley) speak their own dialect and practice a form of Tibetan Buddhism that has some Bon (pre-Buddhist animist religion of Tibet) influences, while the other people of Humla—the Chhetris, whose ancestors came from Persia, Rajasthan, and Kashmir—practice a form of Hinduism. Humla's rich blend of cultures is reflective of its location at the crossroads of ancient trans-Himalayan trade and pilgrimage routes.

We learned from Tenzin that it is proper etiquette to arrive bearing gifts of spiritual significance for the dhamis when we arrive in Humla, as those items will hold a place of honor on their altars and will, in essence, be an offering to the entire village. So we navigated through the crowded, narrow streets and alleyways of the Thamel district in rickshaws in search of gifts. Our driver whirled us past a myriad of businesses catering to Western tastes, where one could find anything from pizza to pasta. The alley was lined with the brightly colored knockoffs of well-known outdoor gear brands.

We arrived at TT Gallery, a store owned by a Tibetan friend of Tenzin's. Every inch of the place was filled with boxes, stacked from floor to ceiling, containing plastic-wrapped ritual objects and icons of Buddhist and Hindu deities. Our mission was to choose ten perfect *drilbus,* intricately designed bronze hand bells that are the most cherished items used in ritual by the dhamis. Tenzin explained, "The drilbu symbolizes the feminine aspects of wisdom and emptiness. Its sound is like impermanence." Each drilbu we chose had to be superior in craftsmanship and perfect in tone. Tenzin inspected several with great care and listened intently for a tone that was deep, resonant, and consistent—what he called "a true sound." At first, I couldn't fathom how to distinguish a bad bell from a good one, but after about an hour of intent listening, I realized that it wasn't just a matter of hearing; I could actually feel "a true sound." It would lull me into an incredible state of calm. Going from the overstimulation of all the day's events, sights, and sounds to the simple clean tones of the ritual bells, I felt my entire body relaxing as if it were experiencing a big long exhale—a taste of timelessness and impermanence.

We began day 2 by venturing to the eastern edge of Kathmandu to visit the sacred grounds of Pashupatinath. Named for the Hindu god Pashupati, also known as Lord Shiva, Pashupatinath is a sprawling complex of stone temples, shrines, and statues whose main temple overlooks the banks of the holy Bagmati River, a tributary of the great Ganges. Although only Hindus may enter the great temple, we were able to appreciate the grandeur of its pagoda-style architecture and the glitter of its golden roof from across the river, as well as stroll through the walkways, steps, and sacred altars throughout the lush landscape of the grounds. Although Pashupatinath is a place where pilgrims and spiritual seekers visit, there are many ascetics and holy men who make their homes within the complex, shunning worldly comforts and living off the alms of visitors.

One of the residents we met was the Singing Saddhu, who expresses his devotion through music. Unlike most ascetics, who have a gruff or unkempt appearance, the Singing Saddhu was a vision of utter beauty, with smooth shiny skin, delicate bone structure, gentle deep-set eyes, perfectly coiffed black hair pulled up in a chignon on top of his head, and a radiant smile. Draped in flowing robes, he moved across the small wooden stage with the grace of a geisha. The androgynous nature of his appearance seemed to underscore the theme of the sacred balance of male and female symbolized by the many lingams—the phallic symbol of Shiva's power— erected throughout the grounds. Although at first glance lingams may be associated with the male sexual organ, the deeper meaning is the joining of male and female energies in the power of creation, as lingams are always balanced on a round disk or pedestal representative of the yoni (female sexual organ). Accompanied by his stringed instrument, the Singing Saddhu gave us a song dedicated to Krishna as a blessing for our journey ahead. As we listened to the Saddhu's serenade, we could see, through a decorated wooden doorway of the courtyard, a perfectly shaped solid oval rock, balanced vertically, that was about three feet high and a foot in diameter. The large lingam was laced with offerings of marigolds, rose petals, and rice. A man whispered a prayer and poured a small bowl of milk over it. As he walked away, a monkey jumped onto the lingam and helped itself to the offerings.

Another colorful resident we hoped to have an audience with was the Milk Baba. Close to eighty years old, this holy man had subsisted on only goat milk and tea since the age of eighteen—an act of commitment toward his practice of being free from desire, free from anything other than the thirst for God. Along with several devotees, we were invited into his small shrine room where he lived and hosted spiritual seekers from all over the world. Its walls were lined with images of deities from many religions. I was mesmerized by Milk Baba's kind face as he spoke of the universality of all religions and the significance of going on pilgrimage, but then found myself distracted by his beaming smile full of beautiful white teeth. I had questioned how healthy it could be for someone to live only on goat milk, but then realized that his special diet was really doing wonders for his teeth. In fact, rather than being emaciated or unhealthy like one would expect someone who only ate milk and tea to be, Milk Baba was incredibly radiant and vital. Luckily he couldn't read my mind, because he may have found its meanderings to be disrespectful. Milk Baba continued our teaching by leading us outside to a mural of him standing next to the pyramidal peak of Mount Kailash in Tibet—one of the holiest pilgrimage sites for Hindus, Buddhists, Bonpos, and Jains—known as the universal center where heaven and earth meet. When he was done speaking, he surprised us all by removing his turban, which was not cloth but actually his *juptas* (dreadlocks) coiled above his head. His unfurled locks were greater in length than his height and trailed behind him like a bride's train. They were a magnificent symbol of his renunciation of worldly life and his connection to the heavens.

Walking across the footbridge of the Bagmati River, we witnessed several cremation ceremonies on the ghats lining the river's banks. It was a strange gift to observe something that felt as if it should be a private affair. In the West we are relegated to looking at our dead covered with make-up in satin-lined boxes before the body is buried enclosed, or burned in a stranger's facilities. Here, a young man near collapse openly wailed while family and friends braced him as they helped him to circle the body wrapped in cloth. The body, resting on a bed of stacked wood, was set on fire, and the smoke of the pyre carried the scent of burned remains. The ashes were scattered into the river of life, so the soul could begin anew. I gazed across the river and realized how seamlessly the sacred and the mundane coexist here, as a bank of camera lenses captured the scene and upriver a woman, bathing topless, washed her hair.

From the density of Kathmandu, we traveled to the stillness of Humla. With the words *Buddha Air* on the tail and wings of our airplane, I somehow felt a sense of security and anticipation of auspicious events to come. As we left the noise, crowds, and polluted air of Kathmandu and approached the Himalayas, I could see Thomas's face soften, his armor fall away, as he spoke of the landscape we would traverse and the healers we would meet. We talked further about my public mission, to capture healing arts around the world before they evolve completely out of existence, and of my private quest to learn what it is to know oneself as a healer. I confessed that I wasn't just making a film, but exploring my family's healing heritage and my own ambivalence regarding my role in its preservation or continuation. It seemed as we got farther from the whirlwind that was Kathmandu and moved into the expansiveness of the majestic peaks, there was more room for openness and honesty between us. Thomas released his role as gatekeeper, I released my role as the filmmaker trying to capture everything in sight, and we began to see each other as fellow travelers who were not merely interested in the somewhat predictable nature of a trekking adventure but who were seeking to perhaps catch a glimpse of the unknowable. As the pilot began our descent, I saw the terraced fields of Simikot and the thin brown line that was our landing strip. Simikot is Humla's connection to the outside world, with its dirt airstrip, public telephone service, and governmental offices. Although this village sits at about 9,600 feet elevation, it seemed a tiny ledge peeking out from between the skirts of the surrounding mountains.

At the landing strip, our local guides, translators, and trekking crew greeted us with shy smiles. They were ready to work. I was ready for a nap. I took advantage of the downtime by sitting and chatting with some villagers, as Thomas filled out the necessary paperwork and went over the itinerary with the team. Our Humla plan would entail traveling on foot from village to village, at elevations of 9,000 to 11,000 feet. Although this was not Everest, for someone who had lived at sea level for twelve years, this was daunting. We would pass through Simikot, climb up to spend our first night in Baraunse, continue our ascent the next day to Torpa, and try to make it to Limitang by nightfall. We'd then start heading down to the village of Bargaun on the third or fourth day, and complete our trek by circling back to Simikot to catch our flight out. Thomas couldn't guarantee that we'd be able to witness a healing ceremony during our brief visit, but he felt we could at least meet the healers and begin a dialogue.

When it was time for us to head out and up, one of the village mothers who had traveled home from Kathmandu with us gave me a gift. She had been holding and studying my hands while we were visiting and then took from her bag some traditional wool gloves that she'd knitted. There were no fingertips on the gloves, as these were meant to be worn for work, so the fingers could remain nimble while the hand was protected from the cold. Through one of the translators she said that my hands were too delicate for the harsh climate of the Himalayas and she made me promise to wear the gloves, especially at night. I put them on right away and when she saw that they fit perfectly, she smiled with pride. I watched her scurrying away in the direction of her home, while I slowly padded my way toward the outer edges of Simikot.

When we reached the outskirts of Simikot, we were greeted by Taka Bahadur Rokaya. He was the first dhami the film crew and I would meet. Taka Bahadur had not seen Thomas in several years, but rushed to greet his friend, expressing his joy, "Aha-ha-ha! … aha-ha-ha! … aha-ha-ha-ha!"

That was basically as much as I could follow of their conversation.

Actually, that's not entirely true. Although I could not understand the words, some things were perfectly clear—like the intimacy of their teasing while they held hands, or the concern in Taka's voice when he pointed at Thomas's throat, which was reddish, or the self-consciousness I felt when Taka pointed at me and started laughing, with some of the other villagers joining in. When Thomas finally had the opportunity to translate for me, I found out that Taka Bahadur had asked if Thomas had brought his second wife—not as in the one you get after you divorce the first one, but the one you get in addition to the first.

"No, she's not mine," Thomas had insisted, but that didn't seem to deter the dhami's teasing. Thomas tried to explain, "She's my friend—she's also a *dhamini*" (female shaman, healer). Thomas and Taka Bahadur then continued with their laughter and banter while I pondered what made me feel more uncomfortable, being thought of as Thomas's concubine or being introduced as a dhamini. I still didn't know much about these shamans and their practices and I definitely didn't feel it was appropriate to be introduced as if I were like them. And I felt what I'd shared with Thomas on the plane was to remain private, not to be announced to strangers.

"You should take photographs of me in my new clothes. What's the use of taking them in such old clothes?" Taka Bahadur protested when he noticed our cameras aimed in his direction. Although he had never seen small video cameras before, he was familiar with a pointed lens because Thomas had taken some portraits of him in the past. Out of habit, we had arrived with guns ablaze, not having taken into account what it might feel like to be caught on camera in our house frocks in front of strangers— even if they had arrived with a dear friend. It was a good reminder for us to be mindful of not only our presence as guests, but also to always ask permission before shooting.

We climbed two wooden ladders to the top level of Taka Bahadur's home. He invited us to sit with him outside his shrine room. His place was typical of the local three-level construction, made of stone, mud mortar, and wood beams. The first level houses the farm animals and the *nagas* (snake spirits), the second is for the main living area and kitchen, and the third level contains the sleeping quarters.

Taka Bahadur had returned from changing and was now dressed in a black overcoat and jewelry appropriate for receiving guests, and was eager to chat. "These were given to me by the villagers when I became their dhami," he said, proudly displaying his gold hoop earrings, silver bracelets and anklets, and his white cloth turban. Taka Bahadur, like all dhamis, performs his healing as a trance medium, channeling the energies of deities or local spirits to help others overcome difficulties and diseases of the mind and body. A dhami's duties also include propitiating spirits and predicting events, as well as advising on auspicious times to travel, plant crops, or marry. This entails performing invocation chants and prayers to call the spirit of the deity forward, and then going into trance while the Shakti (God-energy) enters the dhami's body. The deity then speaks and acts through the medium, and the dhami has no conscious memory of what has transpired during the time he is in trance.

Although he seemed in perfect health, Taka Bahadur told us that he was seeking someone to whom he can pass his mantle, and that he had begun to say his exit prayers in preparation for death. "I am old now. I would like to make one more pilgrimage with you, Thomas, to Lake Manasarovar and Mount Kailash before I die," he said, putting his hand on Thomas's forearm. The dhamis believe that making the arduous pilgrimage into Tibet and bathing in the sacred waters of Lake Manasarovar, in the shadow of Mount Kailash, purifies them and empowers the local deities they channel. When I asked Taka Bahadur why he wished to go with Thomas, he replied, "Because we have history together. Because Thomas is a good friend." Expressing his desire to leave a lasting legacy, Taka Bahadur added, "And because he is a photographer and can photograph me in trance at the lake to show others that I am a real dhami."

Going on pilgrimage is one of the few occasions when a dhami is allowed to leave his community; otherwise they are seen as belonging to their village and local deity and thus are required to stay close to home. This was the only thing Taka Bahadur did not like about his life as a dhami. But, he said, "I've surrendered to my calling. I have given my *ballah* (anklets) to my altar."

I asked Taka Bahadur where he would go if he could. "I wish to visit your country one day. I would like to see what you grow there. I would like to know how I would be welcomed, but I would anger my deities if I left here, so I can't go," he said wistfully. Before we left, Joseph showed Taka Bahadur some of the footage we had shot of him. Looking through the tiny viewfinder of our video camera, Taka Bahadur and the village kids giggled as they saw, for the first time, moving images of the dhami. We didn't have the opportunity to visit Taka Bahadur again, but I sometimes imagine myself, accompanied by friends and family, welcoming him with a Grand Slam breakfast and hitting the road for a trans-American pilgrimage to farms great and small.

It was late afternnoon by the time we headed toward Baraunse, the first of the Nyimba villages. The October air was cool and crisp, but the sun still felt warm on our bodies. I looked up at the sharp peaks bathed in deep saturated blue and it began to sink in that I was really here in the Himalayas. In the distance, women carried baskets of grain strapped to their heads, with their *dzos* (yak-cows) walking beside them. We crossed paths with children shepherding goats who made room for us by coaxing their charges over the steep edge as we passed through the veil of their dust clouds. Farther up the narrow trail, we stepped aside for a man who was behind us, carrying a newly carved log ladder about eight feet long across his shoulders. He smiled as he passed.

We were at about 9,800 feet elevation and it was a relatively easy, steady climb—a good way to get acclimated for our first day. Although stopping to shoot the scenery slowed down our travel time, I was grateful for the opportunities to take in the beauty, enjoy the quietude, and catch my breath in the clean but thinner air. I heard Cora reminding me, "Exhale twice. Inhale once." She had trekked in high altitudes many times and explained that this would prevent me from hyperventilating—a common occurrence with inexperienced trekkers who have the tendency to continually gasp for air in an effort to get more oxygen while forgetting to exhale.

Coming across some cairns that looked like mini stone houses indicated that we were at the edge of Baraunse. Overlooking the village, we could see a cluster of multilevel rectangular homes terraced into a steep hillside and surrounded by fields. We found the next dhami we were coming to visit, Sonam Gyalpo, by spotting the large trident posted on his rooftop, the common indicator of a dhami's home.

Sonam, who must have been in his late twenties or early thirties, was the youngest of the Humla dhamis. His short, black, curly hair peeked out from under a wool cap rather than a turban. He was extremely shy but welcoming, immediately inviting us for tea in the kitchen and living area of his home. Climbing down a ladder from a hole in the rooftop, we were plunged into the darkest and smokiest room I had ever been in. As is typical of homes in this area, for insulation purposes, the kitchen has only one small square window for light and ventilation. Many of the local women suffer a constant cough from the many hours spent in these smoky and dusty spaces.

Having come in from the bright afternoon light, we were operating nearly blind as we fumbled to set up a camera and sound gear. Seeing nothing but black, Joseph asked Karel to try to eke out more light with a reflector, but there wasn't much for it to reflect. Someone grabbed my foot while searching for the microphone. I leaned back into someone's chin trying to find the wall. We finally surrendered to settling down and feeling our way to our seats by crawling along the rug on the dirt floor. When our eyes adjusted and we were at last able to see something, we could make out the silhouette of Sonam seated next to Thomas, the outline of Sonam's wife working at the woodstove in the middle of the room, and the glow of the embers. The cameras were able to pick up more in low-light situations than our naked eyes, so it wasn't until we reviewed the footage and photos later that we realized, in addition to the dhami and his wife, there was a roomful of kids quietly staring wide-eyed at their overexcited guests.

Karel and I had some romantic notions about drinking yak butter tea, as if partaking in this ancient custom would somehow authenticate our Himalayan experience. We were very excited when Sonam's wife poured hot water into a butter churn that contained tea leaves and yak butter.

Having had some experience with this, Cora advised us to drink the tea with moderate pacing. It is customary to keep the guests' cups filled, so drinking our tea too quickly would put pressure on the host to continually fill our cups, while drinking too slowly could insult the host, and would cause the tea to cool and the yak butter to congeal and separate to the surface. As Sonam's wife repeatedly moved the plunger up and down, she joked with Thomas and Sonam about the local belief that the way a woman churns yak butter tea hints at her skills as a lover. After the first few sips, I could see the white of Karel's teeth—the big grin I would come to depend on throughout our travels, and I decided that if I thought of the salty creamy tea as soup, rather than as a beverage, it was actually quite satisfying.

Thomas then explained to Sonam our project to document healing traditions in Humla and our desire to witness a healing ceremony. Sonam assured us we would be invited should there be a need for his healing work, but added, "I have been very busy with farm work, and there has been very little illness in the village." He hadn't been called to perform a healing ritual in three or four months. It seemed unlikely that we would be able to shoot Sonam in trance during our visit, but he kindly agreed to an on-camera interview the following morning.

Taking advantage of the remaining daylight, we decided to catch a glimpse of village life. We found a middle-aged couple hard at work digging a hole about three feet deep and equally wide, with a fire beside them. Preparing the storage of cattle fodder for the winter, they layered slices of dried turnip into the hole that was lined with cornhusks and later sealed with ash and dirt. Continuing down a narrow lane between houses, we found ourselves in the middle of a herd of goats returning home after a day of grazing. In the chaos of the mass homecoming, the din of bells, shepherd whistles, desperate calls of nanny goats in search of their kids, and the babies' responding bleats suddenly engulfed us.

It was pleasant to meet some of the villagers who greeted us with smiles and kindness. The only exception was the other village dhami, with whom we did not schedule a meeting. As he passed by, I caught his scornful look. I was later told he was deliberately giving me the "evil eye." Apparently, he'd been insulted that we did not ask to interview him, even though he had been a dhami longer than Sonam had been. Although I felt sensitive to the idea of offending someone, it was a great reminder that like my teacher in Seattle, healer or not, these people are prone to human frailties like the rest of us—jealousy, fear, ego struggles.

At nightfall, I was happy to retire to our tents, which had been pitched outside on the upper level of Sonam's home. Having been up since 4:30 a.m., flying, trekking, and shooting, I was beyond ready to sink into my sleeping bag. Just as I was relishing settling in, though, we got word that we needed to gear up: the dhami had unexpectedly been summoned and was already on the move toward the patient's home. It did not feel right to be excited that someone was ill and in need of healing, but the opportunity to witness and record our first dhami ceremony was thrilling enough to make me forget about my fatigue.

We scrambled in the dark between houses and along a dirt path. All that was visible were the narrow patches revealed by flashlight beams. Arriving at the patient's home, we entered the already crowded kitchen and living area. Surrounding the patient, Gelkit, were her three husbands, several children, and mother-in-law. As is traditional for many Humlis, Gelkit practices a form of polyandry in which one woman is married to all the brothers of a family. This custom helps to control birth rates and to keep family resources centralized. When I realized one woman was responsible for all the domestic needs of several husbands and children, I was not surprised to learn that fatigue was among Gelkit's symptoms. She was also suffering from insomnia, and pain in her stomach, back, and chest.

Nyadak, the *dangri* (dhami's translator, ritual partner), had already started setting the stage by lighting butter lamps—small metal vessels reminiscent of Aladdin's lamp fueled by yak butter, with strips of rolled cloth for wicks. Dangri Nyadak then placed barley grains onto a rug and laid them in the shape of the Tibetan swastika, an ancient, auspicious symbol used for protection and blessings. The dangri began chanting a mantra to invoke the spirit of the deity and to induce the trance state of the dhami. Joseph and Karel had just enough time to hook up the boom microphone and hang a forty-watt battery-powered light bulb, the only lighting source we had brought.

Dhami Sonam yawned and looked as if he were about to fall asleep. Dangri Nyadak's rhythmic invocation began to calm the effects of the adrenaline that had been coursing through me since we got our call to action. Suddenly, Dhami Sonam snorted and shook violently. As his body jerked, his wool cap flew off his head. His arms clasped his crossed legs, which allowed him to remain seated while his body was jolted by the energy coming into him. This happened in two waves. The dangri fell silent. The deity embodied.

The deity could only communicate with gestures through his host because Dhami Sonam had not yet acquired the power of speech while in trance. It's not appropriate for laypeople to speak directly to a god, so the patient must address questions to the dangri. The dangri, serving as intermediary, then translates the deity's prescriptions and instructions to the patient. Through Dhami Sonam's hand signals, arm movements, and head nods, the dangri ascertained the diagnosis: a hungry ghost was attacking Gelkit. When she crossed paths with some women from another village near the grain mill, the phantom parasite jumped from those women and attached to her, causing her illness and disturbances. The prescription included the dhami performing some healing and exorcism procedures, and Gelkit having to make an offering of flour, sugar, yak butter, and a mix of ash and chicken egg to prevent the ghost from returning.

Dhami Sonam removed a shallow black metal ladle that had been heating over coals. Dhamis often demonstrate their trance healing powers by handling a hot ladle or drinking boiling oil from a ritual bell while exhibiting no pain or evidence of burns. Dhami Sonam licked the hot ladle, blew his breath on the patient, and repeated this three times. He then rubbed his foot with yak butter and pressed some barley grains against the hot ladle with his heel, which created a dramatic sizzling and smoking effect. Dhami Sonam stretched out his leg and pushed his heel against Gelkit's chest and stomach, while her mother-in-law steadied her. She let out a slight groan and grimaced. He completed the healing ritual by lightly lashing the patient's head and back with a whip made of wool straps to chase away the ghost. The dangri said that the deity indicated that she would feel well in three days. When the ritual came to an end, Dhami Sonam snorted, jerked violently once, and threw grains in the air. He returned to his body, pulled his hat onto his head, and was free of any memories of what had just occurred.

With the excitement over, weariness began to creep over me again. Jigme, one of our local guides and translators, intercepted me on the way to my sleep sanctuary. "The women of the village are ready to sing for you now," he said, smiling. I had forgotten that earlier we had requested to listen to and record the village women's traditional songs. They had waited patiently for us to return from the healing ritual. There was no way I could refuse them now. Through their kitchen cough, hacking, and laughter, they sang their hearts out. When the *chang* (barley beer) began to flow, I realized our eternal day would continue its run into the night.

When my head did finally hit the pillow, which was really just my rolled up shell jacket, it was hard to fathom that we had only landed in Nepal four days prior. As we moved higher in elevation, we were moving deeper into the mystical. My body was exhausted and all it wanted to do was sleep, but my mind was stretching, bending, and twisting, trying to wrap itself around all the sights, sounds, and people we'd encountered, and this had only been our first day in Humla.

CHAPTER 7

Keys to Shangri-la

Humla, Nepal
(Approaching the Innermost Cave)

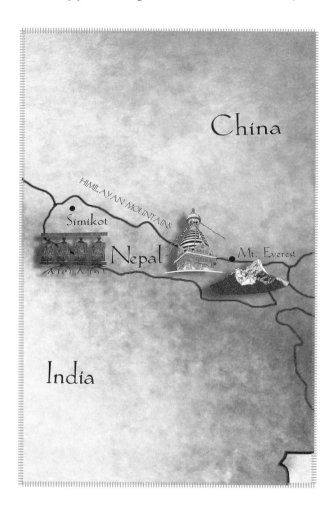

Morning came fast, but its arrival was softened by a trek guide's gentle voice saying, "Morning ... morning," as if it were a question. Once I replied with a groan, a hand carefully slid a cup of steaming chai tea through the zipper of my tent. There was no time to ponder all that had happened in the last twenty-four hours, for we had a long and arduous trek ahead of us. But as my mind awakened, I was suddenly seized by the ridiculous notion that I needed to hurry and direct the shooting of beauty shots, though there is no such thing as an ugly shot in the Himalayas, and I would soon discover that the entire crew had been up and working without me. So much for my attempts at covering up my not being a morning person to this new crew.

After a comforting breakfast of warm flatbread and freshly collected honey, we hit the trail. Our camp supplies, luggage, and heavy gear were loaded onto packhorses and mules, while the supplies we'd need for trekking and shooting were stuffed into our backpacks. Our goal today was to meet the most respected healer in the Humla region, Agu Lama. The physical act of getting to Agu Lama was a test of conviction in itself. We would climb to about 10,300 feet on scant sleep and little time to acclimate to the altitude. I was again feeling the fatigue and the struggle to catch my breath. "Exhale, exhale, inhale. Exhale, exhale, inhale," I reminded myself. My ego was taking a beating, for it seemed I was the only one suffering. I was often trailing far behind, taking up the rear, while Karel, Joseph, and Thomas were happily leading the pack and Cora, along with our five trek guides, bridged the gap in between. At least I knew I wouldn't get lost, as there was only one way to go—up.

Whenever we took breaks along the way, Thomas and our senior guide, Tsering, who was from a nearby village, gave me some CliffsNotes on Agu

Lama and explained why he was held in such high regard. Unlike the other healers we would meet, Agu Lama was not a dhami but practiced as a lama (monk) and *amchi* (doctor). His real name was Lama Tragpa Choden; his title of *agu* (uncle) is one of respect and affection. In the tradition of Padmasambhava, the eighth-century Buddhist saint who brought Buddhism to Tibet by taming the local demons through enlightenment, Agu Lama and his ancestors brought Buddhist practice and thought to this area of Nepal from their homeland of Tibet. Agu Lama's lineage was one of mystics, those who attained the highest levels of spiritual mastery and contemplative states. They were said to engage in intensive practices such as *tummo,* in which they created so much inner heat during meditative states that they could melt snow while wearing only a sheer cotton sheath. In addition to being a meditation master, doctor of Tibetan medicine, and divination master, Agu Lama was also a steward of the ancient sacred Tibetan Buddhist wisdom of *terma,* hidden treasure teachings.

After over five hours of high-altitude hiking, we at last arrived at the chorten, a shrine archway that marked the entrance to Torpa, Agu Lama's village. Within this stone gateway, the ceiling was covered with the vibrant green, red, blue, and gold of intricate paintings of the pantheon of Tibetan Buddhist deities. We passed under the scrutiny of their protective eyes and continued along the trail, which was now lined with *mani* stones inscribed with the Sanskrit mantra *"Om mani padme hum,"* to bless passersby with the power and wisdom of the Buddha of Compassion.

The village center was close, but not yet in sight. I was feeling a bit shaky, but the promise of rest was just around the corner. If I'd had any extra air in my lungs, I might have breathed a sigh of relief, but then Tsering cheerfully announced that we had only another twenty minutes of nearly vertical travel before reaching Agu Lama's actual home. That's when it happened—the meltdown. It came upon me suddenly, the overwhelming feeling of *I can't. I can't take another step. I can't take another breath. I can't direct another shot. I can't do another interview. I can't preserve the healing traditions of the world.* And worse yet, *I can't go home.* I stood in place, frozen, as tears expressing every doubt that had previously been kept at bay came flowing.

Perhaps to help me save face, the crew and trek support team continued to move ahead and left Cora to do her job: corral the out-of-control director. I saw Cora's lips move, but couldn't really hear her. She repeated herself until her words finally pierced through the pall of my inner tirade. "M.-R., you have to eat something. Take a bite of this energy bar," she said, the alarm in her eyes betraying her calm voice. The knot in my belly made the thought of eating seem just as impossible as everything else I currently felt incapable of doing. All I could hear in my head was, *No. I can't.* I didn't realize I had said this out loud, though, until I heard Cora saying, "Yes, you can. You have to. Just take one bite. One bite at a time."

As repulsive as the sweet taste and chalky texture felt in my mouth, I knew Cora was right. I had to. Heeding her advice, I began to feel stronger, clearer. With all the pressures of feeling responsible for the vision of the project, the logistical planning, and the well-being of everyone on the trek, mixed with the physical demands of the journey, I had bonked. Shedding tears was an embarrassing yet efficient way to release, but I then needed to regroup. Cora didn't push me up that last leg. She simply allowed me to find my own pace, my own footing, one step at a time. A flat rock ledge beckoned me to sit and breathe in the view of the valley bathed in the soft afternoon light. The shadows of the mountains above stretched across the village below. For a brief moment, I forgot struggling toward the next destination, the elusive "there," and remembered to just be seated in the "here."

What I previously believed to be simply a cliché was literally true: Spiritual masters are not easily accessible. When I first saw Agu Lama, he was wearing a maroon *chuba* (traditional Tibetan wool coat), large black-rimmed reading glasses with a crack across the middle of one lens, and a cream-colored straw fedora. I was told he was in his late eighties, but he seemed ageless. He was seated on the floor cross-legged before a low table rolling mala beads between his thumb and forefinger, reading text from yellowed rectangular pages that were laid out horizontally across the table.

Thomas leaned over and whispered to me that Agu Lama was throwing a *mo* (divination) for a dhami from the neighboring village of Limitang who was ill and had sent word asking for Agu Lama's assistance. After Agu Lama finished the mo ritual, he greeted the crew and me and invited us to sit before him. Although we were only a few feet apart, there seemed to be a sea of distance between us due to the challenges of language. Agu Lama spoke a Humli dialect that is derivative of Tibetan, which meant we had four layers of translation between us: Tsering explaining the spiritual matters being spoken by Agu Lama to Jigme; Jigme translating from Humli to Nepali to Thomas; and Thomas translating from Nepali to English to me and the crew. Thomas tried to simplify this process by encouraging the camera-shy Jigme, who spoke Humli, Nepali, and English, to be the key translator, but at that time he was lacking the self-confidence to step into that role. Through all the negotiations of language, I felt anxious about how the profound spiritual matters were being conveyed, and what might be getting lost, especially when I was having difficulty following the conversation on practical matters—like where to sleep and eat. To me, being a director had always meant being in control, but with every step on this trek I was being brought to my knees to learn surrender. As I let go of the need to have every word translated and instead simply began to listen and observe, I realized I could follow conversations more easily, intuitively. The truth is, those who wish to be heard make themselves understood, and those who wish to hear make themselves available to listen. And as I did my part, the distance I initially felt was bridged by Agu Lama's openness and warmth as he spoke.

"There is a bit of a negative spell on him," Agu Lama said of Samten, the sick dhami. "The divination reading says he must be suffering a lot." In addition to physical illness, Dhami Samten was apparently also suffering from spiritual illness due to the jealousy of others, the lack of faith in his village, and a breach in his own commitment to his deity. Agu Lama determined that he would have to see the patient to further diagnose his ailments and prescribe herbs for his condition. Thomas, Tsering, Jigme, and Agu Lama were heavily debating whether we should push to make it to Limitang before nightfall to tend to Dhami Samten, or to pace ourselves and wait until morning. Considering the day I had had, I was certain everyone knew which way I would cast my vote. Thankfully, we all agreed it would be best to rest at Agu Lama's overnight.

Our first encounter with Agu Lama was brief, but the day had been long. We pitched our tents on an earthen platform outside the third and highest level of his mud and stone home. Lying in my tent that night, I realized that the ordinary world had shifted somewhere between sea level and the village of Torpa. Exactly when this occurred, I wasn't sure, but it would become more evident as the days elapsed. Despite my sore back, labored breathing, and mental stress, there was a part of me that felt comforted by being in a place where spiritual phenomena was part of everyday life and common conversation. In the middle of the night, I was awakened by Agu's cat meowing as it circled the tent three times.

The following morning, before heading for Limitang, we took a side trip to a small village that was even higher in elevation than Agu Lama's home in hopes of seeing the dhami there. As we made our way up, we ran into a herd of cattle heading down. We were greeted by cattlemen shouting and throwing stones. One was lobbed straight at Joseph, who continued shooting and used his free hand to protect the camera rather than his head—a cameraman's priorities.

Bewildered, we initially thought they might have been upset because we accidentally collided with their cattle drive. Agu Lama's eldest son, Tsewang, the designated leader of this shorter trek, was able to interject himself and speak calmly with the cattlemen. They eventually moved on. Tsewang explained that these villagers had run into another group equipped with cameras that had taken liberties, although members of that group had never asked nor had they been given permission to photograph or approach the dhami. In our case, Tsewang had secured permission in advance, but apparently the villagers had not been notified. Tsewang, an anthropology scholar and community leader, was clearly embarrassed by the situation, but he explained to us that this particular village was more wary of outside influences than the other communities we planned to visit.

Unable to hide his annoyance at their attitude, he told us, "These people are dull—so dull!" This surprised me, but I understood his reaction was perhaps due to his disappointment in our being met with anger rather than openness on his watch. Tsewang's comment made all of us giggle and helped to release some tension, but I walked away feeling this experience was a great reminder that we need to step more lightly when traveling through someone else's field.

We returned to Agu Lama's home, where he had been waiting for us, in time for breakfast. We told him about the morning's excitement, and I mentioned his cat's nighttime visitation. He looked at me and replied matter-of-factly, "The cat was warning you not to go to that village, but you didn't listen." I laughed for I knew he was right. I had felt uneasy about the visit when I woke up, but I chalked up my resistance to being lazy and tired. I was the director, after all, and I convinced myself that I needed to be leading, or at least keeping up with, the rest of the crew. I pressured myself to forge ahead. (Note to self: next time a spiritual master's cat circumambulates your tent meowing, don't just roll over and go back to sleep.)

Despite my failure to read cat admonitions, Agu Lama was still open to sharing his knowledge with me. On our way to Limitang later that morning, Agu Lama led us to a sacred cave, of which he is the guardian and to which he had never given photographic access. He had not mentioned it when we had discussed our travel plans, so the cave was a wonderful surprise. The *bephuk* (hidden cave) was initiated as a power spot in the eighteenth century by Agu Lama's grandfather, Lama Kushog Lunbo. Since then, the responsibility of caring for the cave, maintaining the knowledge of its significance, and protecting its contents has fallen to his descendants.

Agu Lama unlocked the padlock on the wooden door that sealed the cave entrance with a key that hung by a string around his neck. Before we entered, he pointed to the outline of an imprint above the door, which he said was the figure of Padmasambhava wearing a hat—evidence of the great saint's presence and a symbol of the sacred nature of the cave. Legendary

Photos by Cora E. Edmonds

Don Pablo Amaringo teaching children to paint the rain forest, Peru

Director of photography Joseph Hudson and sound guy Matthew G. Monroe, Hawaii

The author with Papa K, Hawaii

Papa K making an offering to the volcano goddess, Pele, above a steam vent, Hawaii

Uncle Robert welcoming us to his Hawaiian Nature Walk

Nancy Kahalewai and Aunty Mary

Aunty Mahealani, Hawaii

Dangri Tsering serving two dhamis—Dhami Mangale and Dhami Sher Bahadur, Humla, Nepal

Director of photography Joseph showing kids footage we'd shot of them, Humla, Nepal

Milk Baba has subsisted on only his faith and goat milk for over six decades, Kathmandu, Nepal

Ani taking a tea break from the ceremony, Ladakh, India

Ladakh Landcape

Our host family: Dawa, his wife, Thinles Angmo, and their daughter Diki, Ladakh, India

Karel, Thomas, Joseph, and the author rest in host family's "best room," Ladakh, India

Naxi Dongba performing a ceremony, Lijiang, China

Texts with Naxi pictographs, Lijiang, China

A Humli woman cooking in a typical kitchen by the light of a single window

Photos by Thomas L. Kelly

Rainbow over Humla Valley, Nepal

Agu Lama in his sanctuary, Humla, Nepal

Dhami Mangale, Humla, Nepal

Dhami Samten, Humla, Nepal

Dhami Sonam, Humla, Nepal

Terraced homes in Humla, Nepal

Village of Simikot in Humla, Nepal

Boudhanath Stupa, Nepal

Prayer Wheels, Kathmandu, Nepal

Pashupatinath temple, Nepal

Dhami Taka Bahadur, Humla, Nepal

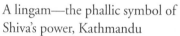

A lingam—the phallic symbol of Shiva's power, Kathmandu

Shiva and Parvati, Kathmandu

Dhamis and dangris emerge after a sacred bath in Lake Manasarovar, Tibet

Sacred Mount Kailash, Tibet

An amchi making offering before the Medicine Buddha altar, Ladakh, India

Amchis and lamas during the medicine potentization ceremony, Ladakh, India

Amchi with medicinal herbs and text, Ladakh, India

Imbibing the potentized medicine, Ladakh, India

Lama Rigzin leading the medicine potentization ceremony, Ladakh, India

Purification nectar

Nectar poured over a mirror for cleansing impurities, Ladakh, India

Decorating tormas, Ladakh, India

Self-portrait of photo-activist Thomas L. Kelly

Photo by Thanh Lêquang

Aunty Lien, the author's aunt and a
Vietnamese spiritual healer

imprints like this are found in many places considered holy by Tibetan Buddhists, and reveal an enlightened being's mastery over the material world—the ability to alter the density of stone into malleable matter.

Inside the cave was a statue of Padmasambhava surrounded by eight miniature conical towers containing religious relics. Agu Lama began to speak with a passion and urgency we hadn't yet witnessed from him, and Tsewang, who was translating for his father, had difficulty keeping up. Agu Lama was animated, his voice expressive and melodious. "It is believed that many keys to the *beyul* (hidden valleys, secret paradises) are hidden here," he said.

"What do you mean by the keys?" I asked eagerly.

Agu Lama pointed to his flat hand and said, "They are texts that explain the hidden valley, where it is, how it is—and the keys will indicate when it is the time to reveal the secret paradise."

Tsewang clarified his father's message: in the eighth century, Padmasambhava and his consort, Yeshe Tsogyal, placed keys to heavenly realms, or magical kingdoms, in caves throughout the Himalayas. They did so with the hope that they could be accessed here on earth at a later time. These keys were to be discovered by highly evolved sages in a future time of rampant famine, disease, and war. The sages, or *tertons* (treasure discoverers, revealers), are the chosen ones who can decode and reveal the meaning of the keys. Within the hidden treasure teachings are instructions on how to reach the beyul, where the blessed would be led to a paradisiacal existence. In essence, these keys, or treasure teachings, could be likened to a time capsule of sacred information set aside for future generations to discover.

"So these days, are there any treasure discoverers to reveal the hidden valleys?" Tsewang asked his father.

"When the time is not yet ripe, it's not beneficial to open the hidden treasure. When the right time and the need to reveal the hidden valley coincide, then it will be beneficial," Agu Lama replied.

As we left the cave, he added, "These days, people just go around seeing and taking photographs of the external landscape only. They don't know the inner meaning that exists." I asked Agu Lama if these hidden valleys,

secret paradises, or magical kingdoms are actual physical places or meta-
phors for a metaphysical state of being. His answer was, "Yes."

Agu walked aided by his cane and Tsewang's arm much of the way from
the cave to Limitang, but he finished the journey on his donkey. As they
ambled up and down, traversed switchbacks, and crossed creeks, Agu Lama
patted the donkey's neck and whispered mantras and thanks in its ear.
When we arrived, Tsering, who had gone ahead the previous evening,
asked, "Why are you so late? We've been waiting for you."

Saying nothing of our excursion to the cave, Agu Lama replied, "We
talked about different things, and it took some time."

The ailing Dhami Samten and Agu Lama greeted each other by bowing
and touching foreheads. Dhami Samten seemed frail in his worn, oversize
sport coat and blue sweatpants. Nevertheless, he greeted us with kind
eyes and a quiet smile. Sitting beside each other, the two friends discussed
Samten's illness. Using a Tibetan medicine diagnostic technique, Agu Lama
took his friend's pulse reading by pressing his fingers on the radial artery of
Dhami Samten's wrist, while the dhami described his symptoms. Unlike
trance healing, in which the deity chooses the dhami, who goes through
no formal training, a doctor of Tibetan medicine is required to attend
decades of schooling to be certified as an amchi.

Just as Agu Lama had divined, Dhami Samten had been suffering con-
siderably with back pain, stomach pain, and diarrhea. He had been given
various treatments and medications, but said to Agu Lama, "Except for
yours, other medicines don't seem to work well. The [Western] medicine
from the [government] health post doesn't work at all. I went several times."

"It's bile and wind systems," Agu Lama announced, releasing Dhami
Samten's wrist. In Tibetan medicine, like in traditional Chinese medicine,
bodily functions are governed by three systems or humors: bile, wind, and
phlegm. When the humors are out of balance, illness occurs. Agu Lama
reached into his medicine bag, a faded canvas sack, and unwrapped *rigzin
rilbu* (peppercorn-size round pills) and olive-colored powder from folded
paper packets. He used a small spoon to scoop the powder into a cup of

boiled water and instructed Dhami Samten to take it in three doses. "You can't have buckwheat pancakes, and not too much barley beer," he advised. Although Dhami Samten said he had given up chang three years ago, he admitted that he still drinks some *arak,* Humla moonshine.

Despite his not feeling well, Dhami Samten had a strong desire to do a ceremony for us on-camera. He invited us for tea, perhaps to give Agu Lama's medication some time to do its work. Although it was also part of Agu Lama's prescription for Dhami Samten to make offerings and perform rituals to right things with his deity, I worried that this activity wasn't a good idea in light of his condition. But that wasn't for me to decide.

"Go and start your drumming. Shake the valley!" Agu Lama cheered.

In procession, our crew and trek team walked to the sacred ceremony site, followed by a few drummers and the men, women, and children of the village. Excitement was in the air and we sensed this was special for all concerned. The site had an old mud-and-stone chorten that was encircled by a grove of trees. Dhami Samten arrived a few minutes later, now dressed for ceremony in a cotton knee-length wrap tunic and matching pants. He was adorned with jewelry, including gold hoop earrings and several strands of *rudraksha* beads, gumball-size seeds that were rusty in color and bumpy in texture—said to be the tears of Shiva. With pats of sacred yak butter on his temples and a trident in his hand, his costume was complete. Unlike the quiet healing ritual we had witnessed on our first night in Humla with Sonam, who treated his patient with silence and hand signals, this ceremony would be more of a spectacle—a demonstration for us and our cameras.

The drummers lined one side of the shrine area, while Agu Lama, Tsering, and some male elders sat opposite them in front of a stone wall. The villagers congregated behind it. Joseph and Karel, each shooting a camera, had an all-access pass, while the rest of us had front-row seats. Dhami Samten's brother prepared the shrine area just as Sonam's dangri did in the first village. Tsering acted as the dangri for this ceremony, to translate once the dhami went into trance.

The quiet of the wooded shrine was suddenly pierced by the rhythmic beat of the drums, inducing the trance state of the dhami. The tempo moved faster and faster, and this dhami wasn't just going to sit, shake, and wait for the deity to come. Instead, Dhami Samten got on his feet, quivering and dancing with his eyes half closed. He tossed his head back and forth like a rock star, causing his turban to fall, unfurling his long black wavy strands of hair. From his mane tumbled a lock of hair coiled in silver that reached the ground—his antenna to the gods. He stepped from one side of the stage to the other. He put his hands on his hips and hopped. He spread his arms open and spun. And then he fiercely stabbed a trident into the ground center stage. The drumming immediately stopped. All was still.

Jieptak, the deity for whom this shrine was named, was now present in Dhami Samten. He seated the dhami's body and addressed us in the verse of gods, "*Ah hey! Ah hey!* Listen! Listen! Now at this time, you in the material world!" The deities of this area speak an archaic language and use poetry, parable, and metaphor to advise humans. It was the job of the dangri, whose calling is handed down from father to son, to create the necessary link to make this spiritual language accessible to the mostly uneducated laypeople in the form of common words and phrasing. Because I wanted to experience the deity's art of language, we were lucky to be able to get true translations rather than simply the abbreviated version.

As is customary with these channeled deities, Jieptak opened with his commitment and origination story, in which he declared his promise to help in the human realm and described from where he has traveled to be embodied through Dhami Samten here and now:

Ah hey! Today
You must maintain your commitment
To us, the wind bodies
When I say commitment
I do not need the best
I do not need the most colorful
Today

Ah hey! I, today
From the corner of the valley of Lunghphuk

I, the spirit living among the rocks
Reaching through to this decadent age
Today

Bound by the oath to
My dharma friend [Padmasambhava]
To serve beings in the material world
Living on offerings
Of milk, barley beer, and grains
Such is my fate
Today

Ah hey! Now, today
About my dwellings of the past
In the eastern side of the valley
I dwelled
In the plains of the Lungphuk Valley
Now, these days
On the bottom of the Gungling Hill
I still dwell
In my hermitage
Today

Ah hey! Now, today
Due to my oath
To my dharma friend [Padmasambhava]
I have come to this fate
Today

The deity continued by sharing his worry over the loss of the dhami tradition, the result of the dilution of spiritual essence in the world.

I'm concerned about a time in this material world when there will be no cures through exorcism and channeling. It is the decadent age. If you add a bowl of water to a bowl of milk, what becomes of it? If you add two bowls of water to a bowl of milk, what becomes of it? And if you add two pitchers of water to that same bowl of milk—how much of the white of the milk is lost?

After the teaching, the deity began the divination. Tsering asked about the possibilities of going on a sacred pilgrimage. Jieptak replied, "If you were to speak of single-pointed faith, body, and soul as ever-present as Mount Kailash and as calm as Lake Manasarovar, I do not find that level in all of them," he said, pointing to me and my crew. The deity then questioned our sincerity in participating in the sacred, implying our intention may be one of mere curiosity or of testing the deity's powers, rather than respecting his advice and abilities. Admittedly, I had been enjoying the experience more as entertainment than as a profound spiritual experience. The showmanship and staged feel of the spectacle made me question the authenticity of spiritual integrity behind the events. As a director, though, it made for colorful footage. I had no idea how personal things were about to get.

Not condemning us entirely, Jieptak, via Dhami Samten, told us that although we were not ready today, if we were to commit to the spiritual path, then it would be possible to depart for the journey on the first day of the sixth month of the Tibetan calendar, eight months from now. He handed some barley grains wrapped in cloth to Dangri Tsering and said, "*Ah hey!* These grains I have given, keep them with you and watch your dreams for three days. You of the material world today ... should not be so proud ... just because you can fly over the land through the sky, does not mean you can escape spiritual commitments and karma [laws of cause and effect]." Pointing at me, he continued, "This one, tell her to keep the grains under the pillow and wait for that dream." Tsering clarified the deity's message and handed the small bundle to Jigme, who'd seemed to have gotten past his shyness a little bit by now, because he placed it in the palm of my hand and translated for me. In English, Jigme said, "If there is to be success in your work, you will have a dream of fruition. If there are to be obstacles, you will have a bad dream." Up to that moment I had been spacing out, just enjoying the show. As usual, Joseph and Karel were competently recording the event, the dhami was giving us a great performance, so I didn't have to be on. I was caught off-guard at being addressed directly, the unwitting audience member pulled onstage into the spotlight. Despite the embarrassment I felt, I was also touched by the acknowledgment and inclusion.

After the ceremony and the dinner that followed, Agu Lama reviewed for us the essence of Dhami Samten's channeled teaching. "In the beginning, there was only the harmless path. Now the level of spiritual rule in the material world is diminished." He added that the rampant lack of spiritual commitment and compassion is setting the stage for a bleak future, and then explained the principle of karma. "There is the saying, 'What you did in the past is what you receive now. What you will receive in the future is what you do now.' It is like your land. If you plow your land and sow your fields properly, you will get good crops later." He closed with, "We, the people of the material world, must never abandon these things."

Taking into consideration all that transpired during the ceremony, I went to sleep that night questioning my spiritual commitment, faith, and fears. Although the deity had addressed all who were present, it was clear that he was speaking to the universal as well as the personal—or more accurately, to me personally. I was still stubbornly holding on to my belief that I could remain an observer of the spiritual world and not an actual participant. Once again, I was surprised to realize that I could be so clearly seen when I believed that it was I who was doing the observing. The deity had apparently picked up on my insecurities and fear of failure, and had given me a tool to look within myself for the answer.

It would take me years to grasp the importance of being seen without being judged over the course of my journey. With every observation a healer would make about my challenges (or what I perceived to be my flaws), I was also given a remedy. It was clear that to truly understand the world of these spiritual healers, I would have to be willing to step through the doorway into their reality. And yet, I held that one foot out as long as I could for that part of me wasn't quite ready to give up the comfort of familiarity. And it knew that once I committed, there would be no turning back.

It was only day 3 in the Himalayas. The air got thinner and thinner, as did the veils between the practical and mystical world, the observer and observed, waking and dreaming. I placed my seed bundle under my pillow that night and wondered if the dream would happen at some point over the next three nights. Somewhere between fading mental meandering and morning light, it came. *I am trekking into Tibet toward sacred Mount Kailash—the axis mundi where Heaven and Earth meet. Its four-sided peak pierces the blue sky. The white of the snowcap kisses a single cloud. Jigme, our translator and guide, walks toward me in slow motion, smiling.*

CHAPTER 8

Event Horizon

Humla, Nepal (the Ordeal)

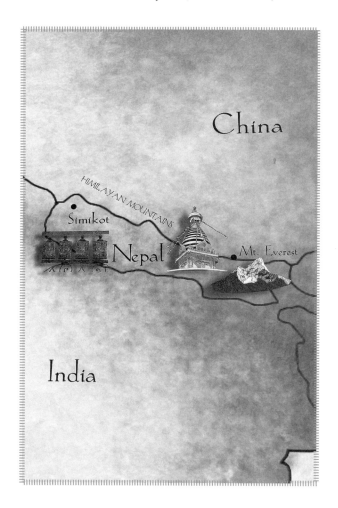

It was supposed to be all downhill from here. The thought of that made me outright giddy. We'd been privileged to witness many sacred rituals, meet generous and kind people, and visit special places, and we'd shot more video footage than expected. As much as I enjoyed the Humla adventure, the trekking part had truly been a grueling effort for me. Now, as we headed toward Bargaun, the last village, with plans to shoot there for only half a day the following morning and then circling back to where we started in Simikot, I felt I could relax and exhale. We would be descending about 1,700 feet in elevation and I was elated by the idea of an easy jaunt. As it turned out, we were running out of daylight, so our guides told us in order to make it before nightfall, we would actually have to sprint down the mountain, and rather than following the established switchbacks, we would have to go off-trail and make a beeline for our destination. They said it should take less than an hour if we moved fast. Well, what takes our local experts less than an hour would take me an hour and a half. My knees, especially the one with the ACL repair, had already been complaining about trekking up; now they were moaning loudly, as bouncing down was decidedly worse. Oh, to have had hiking poles then!

I didn't make it to Bargaun before nightfall, but there was something incredibly peaceful about the stillness of trekking after the sun goes down. I had to be mindful with each step, and despite having no help from an emerging new moon, my eyes seemed to adjust with the fading light. There weren't many trees, so there was no fear of running into any dangling branches or hidden trunks. It would most likely be tripping over brush and slipping on rocks and scree that would be my demise if I wasn't careful. In order to avoid injury or missteps, I focused solely on my immediate surroundings and on what lay directly ahead. It was a great practice of presence.

Before I ever spotted the village, I knew we were close from the smell of smoke in the air as evening meals were being prepared in the kitchens below. When we arrived in the village, Tsering said something gruffly to Jigme, the poor guide who seemed to be stuck with me a lot, that sounded like, "What took you so long?" Jigme didn't bother to translate, nor did he point a finger at the slowpoke with the creaking knees standing behind him. He simply bowed his head and sounded like he was apologizing. Tsering, our lead guide and now our host in his home village, had been a bit more distant and cool with us initially. In fact, on our first night in Humla, after having had a fair amount of chang, he let loose and told us all very loudly how he felt about people coming to his homeland and having the audacity to think his customs and traditions were so simple that they could be understood with just a few days spent passing through. Things got loud when the other Humli team members and villagers tried to shush him because he was embarrassing them in front of their guests. I actually understood how he must have felt and asked Thomas to tell Tsering that I agreed with him. I added that had we been able to procure more funding, we would have relished having more time to be deeply immersed in the local traditions. Our intention wasn't to trivialize the richness of his way of life, but rather to humbly do what we could to learn and share with the resources we had. He sat quietly for a moment and then let out a roar of laughter. Everyone then joined in and it seemed the tension was released for the moment and he continued to slowly warm to us in the following days.

This evening, however, Tsering seemed uptight again. I couldn't tell if this was due to his concern for all his wards arriving safely in the dark or if something else was bothering him. While his team was setting up the sleeping areas for me and the crew in Tsering's home, his wife and daughters were putting the finishing touches on our dinner. We were served warm flatbread and a hearty delicious stew made with local root vegetables and small chunks of dzo meat. Because meat protein is scarce and prized in Humla, especially heading into the winter months, it was a privilege to be given such a gift that is only served on special occasions or to honored guests. After our long day and traveling in the cool of night, we all savored the rich flavors, comfort, and warmth of the stew. It wasn't until he heard all of us uttering sounds of appreciation that a smile crept across Tsering's lips. He explained that he had had previous experiences with visitors who were not aware that refusing his offer of food and eating their own freeze-dried trekker food and energy bars was hurtful and insulting to his family. Little did he know that an unspoken credo of the LBC club was that, as diehard foodies, we only eat local food wherever we travel. Karel sealed his membership into the club when he asked not only for seconds, but thirds as well, pleasing Tsering to no end and causing the women to giggle with delight.

After dinner, while Tsering rolled wicks from strips of cotton cloth for his yak-butter lamps, we learned how he came to be the dangri of two dhamis. Tsering was raised in Bargaun and his father was a dangri. Accompanying his father to various ceremonies and helping him prepare for rituals, Tsering learned the role of the dangri was not only to serve his dhami and his deity, but also to advocate on behalf of the villagers to their spiritual guides—the dhami being the vehicle and the dangri the bridge over which the mystical and physical worlds are traversed. Over time, he learned the special vocabulary of the ancient language of the deities to interpret their expressions of lyrical allegory, simplifying the channeled messages back to those seeking guidance and healing, just as he'd done for us in Limitang.

Tsering wanted a different experience of the world when he reached adulthood and left his village to become a police officer, eventually rising to the rank of constable. His duties took him to other villages in Humla and to Jumla, a larger region with greater prospects. It was a rough-and-tumble occupation witnessing the dark side of human nature—crime, corruption, and violence—but it offered his family a more prosperous lifestyle.

With the passing of his father, Tsering was called back to Bargaun to take his rightful place as the village dangri. Although he initially declined to accept his expected obligation, his family and wife encouraged him to leave his law enforcement career and follow tradition. It was a big sacrifice for him to go back to living on subsistence farming and the occasional trek guide job, but he knew his village needed him and that this previously honored role was disappearing in the Humla valley. Many young men do not make the same choice that Tsering made, causing a shortage of dangris, which was why he served two dhamis and was the pinch-hitter for missing dangris in other villages.

Tsering shared that there was an added incentive, as there were plenty of stories of those who had refused their calling and subsequently fell ill, died in mysterious ways, or had gone mad.

After hearing his story, I understood more clearly why Tsering was so guarded with us at first. For a man who was used to commanding respect as an authority figure, it must have required a great deal of humility to be in service to others as a dangri, and at times to be viewed as being in servitude to arrogant visitors. Smart trekkers understand the importance of respecting and appreciating their guides and porters. They are the fount of knowledge, the strength upon which camps are made and moved, and the lifeline to survival when exploring unfamiliar territory.

In bright morning light on the upper terrace of Tsering's home, Dhami Mangale poured water from a small metal vase onto his finger and ran it along his teeth. He then poured the rest of the water over his feet and rubbed them clean. All this primping was done for our sake, as he was preparing to do a joint ceremony with another dhami, Sher Bahadur, with Tsering as their dangri. Unlike the other ceremonies we'd attended, this would be a quiet, private one done just for us. Since Dhami Mangale was the oldest one in all of Humla, and Dhami Sher Bahadur channeled the most ancient deity, these two had nothing to prove. There would be no divination or healing. They simply wanted to give a short demonstration of their channeling and to give their guests blessings from their deities.

We were once again in the main room of Tsering's home, but this time on the opposite end of where we'd had dinner the previous evening. Although it was daytime, the room was pitch black but for a single shaft of light coming in from a small square window. Tsering's wife and one of his daughters were in the adjacent kitchen space frying eggs and making flatbread. It must have been a full-time job keeping all of us fed. Like most women in Humla, these two also had a persistent cough and soot-covered faces from spending so much time in a mostly enclosed space with an open fire pit. With the permeating smoke filling our lungs and floating above us, we were lulled by the rhythm of the dough being flattened as it was slapped from hand to hand, while Dhami Mangale added to the soundtrack with gentle drumming and chanting to help Dhami Sher Bahadur go into trance.

Once in trance, Sher Bahadur's deity, Gonba Checktuk, began as all the deities do by telling his origination story—having come from the Tibetan Plateau and settling in Bargaun—and then making some commentary on the current state of the human realm. He began his call and response conversation with Tsering and us. He first addressed the issue of people not making efforts to change their own circumstances or to develop themselves:

> *Ah hey!*
> *If one doesn't take three steps through the valleys*
> *And over the seven mountains,*
> *One can't cross over*
> *Isn't this so?*

Tsering responded with, "My prostrations," which in effect meant, "Yes, it's so."

Then he spoke to how people have lost the wisdom to discern friend from foe and have forgotten that we are all of the same family:

> *Ah hey!*
> *If people would remember*
> *That they come from the land of the great father and the great mother*
> *They would understand that when we are destined to be as relatives*
> *We would not lose each other as enemies*

Isn't this so?
But, now, today,
One can't figure out people by raising them
And one can't figure out the birds by the songs they sing today
Isn't that so?

Tsering agreed once again, "Yes, it's so," and then talked to the deity about our work of using media to bring blessings to others in order to spread knowledge about their traditions, and to preserve them for the future. "If we tie a bell to a bird in the sky, the people around the world will hear its ring. If we tie a bell to a rat inside a hole, between the walls its sound will remain. So, we ask for your blessing for their work."

Sher Bahadur's deity obliged and gave us a blessing by putting grains in a bell, directing us to put a *kata* (offering scarf) on Sher Bahadur, and asking Tsering to give me some barley grains. The deity closed with these instructions:

Ah hey!
If you have a stable mind, you will have successful work.
If you all have one mind, you will have success in your work.
So, divide these grains among your people and send them inside
    (swallow them);
Then a stable mind and oneness among you will come.
Not to worry.

Just as Sher Bahadur finished speaking, we were thrown into darkness. I heard people scrambling. Someone passed me a yak-butter lamp. Someone else grabbed it from me and lit it. And we were back in business. All of a sudden the other dhami, Dhami Mangale snorted, his body shook, and he began to channel his deity.

Dhami Mangale's deity, Chokyong Rinpoche, also came from Tibet, but he was more specific in stating that he was from the capital of the ancient Zhang Zhung area, which was the center of the Bon religion that predates Tibetan Buddhism. Having attached himself through the lineage of some families from Zhang Zhung who eventually migrated to Nepal, he came to Bargaun.

Ah hey!
Landing in the shrine of the village of Bargaun,
I act as an agent of warmth when it is wet and of water when it is dry.
But even when you can't find a cave with warmth
And there may be evil spirits spanning all the valleys
I will be there to keep an eye on them, from the realm that is unseen.
Isn't that so?
This land [Humla] is ravaged by negativity and jealousy
You people coming from foreign lands with faith is a welcome thing
Like grains when sifted, the inferior ones will move to the edge,
While the superior ones will remain in the center.
The more we rub the conch shell, the whiter it becomes.
The more we rub the coal, the blacker it becomes.
You will see things that you are not supposed to see
And you will hear things that you are not supposed to hear
While I, a being from the boundary land at the edge of Samsara,
See that this [human] realm will get darker, not brighter.
But even as things get darker
For the one with faith, there will radiate a brilliance and brightness.
Isn't that so?

Tsering responded with, "My prostrations—yes, it is so," and the deity gave us a parting gift of barley grains and instructed me to carry them with me, while assuring that if anything happened on my travels, he would take responsibility, so I needn't worry. The deity closed with, "and even if my vehicle cannot go," referring to Dhami Mangale, who was older and not physically able to travel anymore, "I can go riding on someone else."

Both dhamis came back to their bodies and asked Tsering what had happened. Upon hearing that the deities gave blessings, Sher Bahadur said, "If the deities offered protection, then it is fortunate for the dhamis, the dangris, and all of us. May we all be fortunate!" We finished up with

Thomas and Cora taking some still photographs of the dhamis. Afterward, as is customary in Humla, the men (Thomas, Joseph, Karel, and our trek guides) were invited to share in some chang at a neighbor's home, while the women cleaned up and Cora and I packed in preparation for our departure.

I had been feeling unwell all day with nausea and a persistent headache, so as Cora and I reflected on how fulfilling the trip had been despite its many challenges, we both agreed we were ready to move on from Humla. After we finished packing our things, we were leisurely strolling to gather the men, when all of a sudden I fell to the ground. I hadn't tripped or stumbled, but rather it was as if someone had knocked my legs out from under me. I was light-headed, confused, and had difficulty speaking clearly. I didn't know what was happening, but I knew I was in trouble and needed help. In halting speech, I pleaded with Cora to call for the dhamis.

I've only been irrefutably drunk twice in my life. Once when I had returned to France at the age of twelve and the adults decided I was ready to have grown-up servings of wine with every meal, which meant drinking it straight as opposed to the kiddie watered-down version. During one lunch, my French uncle, Tonton Hubert, thought it would be hilarious to fill my wine glass imperceptibly whenever I wasn't looking, so it seemed as if it were a bottomless glass. Having graduated to adult-ish status, I wanted to show that I could hold my own, so I continued to drink the wine in hopes that I'd at least finish one whole glass of the straight stuff. Needless to say, this did not end well, and I was put to bed with my head spinning, my limbs limp, and muttering utter nonsense that remained the fodder of family jokes for years to come.

The second time I was completely inebriated was when I was twenty-one years old. I was at a nightclub with coworkers after a long evening shift and had been a dancing fool all night. When I returned to our table, I was parched and downed my then boyfriend's Long Island iced tea, not realizing that the "Long Island" meant I was quenching my thirst not with iced tea but with a fully loaded cocktail that contained gin, rum, tequila, vodka, and triple sec. That one ended with my having several intimate conversations with the porcelain goddess, while my ex-boyfriend, later to become my husband, held me up so I wouldn't fall in or over. Those two experiences are the best way for me to describe how I felt after I fell to the ground.

After our team and the dhamis showed up, I remember being collapsed on the ground on the upper level of Tsering's home and sobbing uncontrollably. I have no idea how I got there or why I was crying. Thomas and Cora were behind me with their hands on my back and shoulders steadying me, while Dhami Mangale was on one side of me trying to comfort me; Tsering was on the other side barking orders to his family and the trek guides in an effort gather the tools and medicine needed to help me. What followed lives only in bits and pieces in my memory. Like trying to remember a dream after waking, some of the emotions remain with me, but the details seem to slip farther away the more I try to grasp them. In fact, I really only know the sequence of what the LBC would come to refer to as "the freak-out" from repeatedly reviewing over time the video footage that was taken when Thomas made the call for Joseph and Karel to roll cameras, as he and Cora looked after me. Both Joseph and Karel would later tell me it was one of the most difficult things they ever had to do—maintain their documentarian perspective behind the lens while watching their friend in such distress.

When asked about these events years later, Thomas would say, "When I arrived, I was in shock. I thought she was having an epileptic fit. I was quite worried that something had happened. We are up at a high altitude, could be dehydration, 'cause she was shaking, her eyes were bulged, and her veins were popped out. The dhamis were incredibly concerned. You know, I think that they were also perplexed that this might be a physical illness—as I said, an epileptic fit—but it quickly became very clear to them that this wasn't the case."

The first thing Dhami Mangale called for was holy water from Lake Manasarovar. This was no small offering as this precious commodity is solely gathered on pilgrimage to the sacred lake in Tibet—something that can only be done when the dangris and dhamis have the time, physical stamina, and resources to make the two- to three-week trek. Tsering poured some of the water into my mouth and into my cupped hands. I was lucid enough to understand their instructions to hold my hands out for water, and I took big gulps and then splashed the rest over my face and neck. It seemed to quench my excruciating thirst, and it felt cooling to my throat and soothing on my skin.

I struggled to speak, but when the sounds came out, they were violent exclamations and guttural noises. I felt terrified and frustrated at not being able to control my body nor to express myself. Then I heard Thomas's calm voice saying, "They want to take you inside, M.-R. The dhami wants to work on you in there, okay?" As he, Cora, and Tsering helped me up, Thomas spoke to the camera. "She was speaking a language that none of us understood." I was hoisted onto the back of Rinchinpo, our smallest guide, but apparently one of the strongest, and he heroically carried hysterical me down the wooden ladder to the ceremonial area where we'd shot the two dhamis that morning.

Everyone scrambled to prepare for an exorcism to rid me of whatever they believed had possessed me. Dhami Mangale rang his bell and started to chant to invoke the helpful deities. As I writhed on the floor, I remember feeling whipcords lashing me several times as Dhami Mangale, yelled *"Hey! Hey! Hey!"* with every strike. It didn't hurt. It just felt irritating. Then someone threw barley grains at me several times, which felt like being pelted with a slew of spit wads. Again, this was not painful, but made me feel angry. Then someone put a piece of paper on my head, which I would later learn was a five-rupee bill made as an offering. I clawed at it and threw it aside. Anything touching me felt intolerably agitating.

After assessing that their attempts at exorcism failed, Tsering and the dhamis determined that this was because it was not an evil spirit that had taken over my body, but rather some kind of powerful deity. They then decided to try to reason with it. Tsering opened with, "We welcome the deity, but we request that it not cause pain to her body." I felt exhausted from struggling and finally surrendered the fight to regain control of myself. A feeling of peace came over me as I let go. I was now free to float above, watching someone else swaying on her knees, moving her arms, and using her mouth to speak. Sometimes she spoke in gibberish and other times she spoke in English. "We understand it is difficult to be human," she began, "and to fight the human tendencies of jealousy and untruth and power over. But, you must be pure. You must fight to be pure. All the dhamis must work together and cleanse impurities."

Tsering responded with, "Thank you. Yes, we agree. These people came from far away to pay homage to our deities, and now you appeared here in a body, and we are delighted that we have this opportunity to meet one another. But we beseech you now to leave her body. It's enough, now."

The person inside me cut him off with, "He doesn't tell me when I've had enough. I'll leave soon. She's fine. We appreciate his concern for this one. We are not angry." She then asked for Tsering's and Dhami Mangale's hands and said she was giving them some of her power, so that they may be strengthened in their commitment to lead others with the purity of their hearts. After Tsering promised that the dhamis would pass on her message of spreading positivity and vanquishing jealousy, dishonesty, and darkness, I was jolted back into my body. It felt so heavy that I had no strength to hold it up and I promptly collapsed.

As I gradually came back to consciousness, Dhami Mangale tried to put the pieces of what happened together for everyone. He felt that I must have channeling in my family heritage, which made me more susceptible to being possessed. He also proposed that I may have suffered from betrayal and had grief in my heart, as well as fear in my mind from being in a foreign land where negativity abounded. This must have weakened my defenses. Dhami Mangale said he saw that it was actually two spirits who entered me—first, a local male spirit associated with lower energies, then a higher female deity who most likely originated from the south—which explained why I was fearful and crying at first, but then was more calm later and able to fully surrender. And because my body was left unharmed, it was clear the female deity was a beneficent one. While Dhami Mangale spoke, Tsering watched me becoming more myself again and whispered, "See how her face is changed now?"

When I came to, I opened my eyes to see Joseph with the camera aimed at me. My first words were, "I thought I told you guys to stop shooting. Must save tape … cameras down." Joseph laughed and replied, "Welcome back." I was so relieved that I was able to speak the words I had actually intended to say. It was comforting to see Joseph smile, to feel my head cradled in Thomas's arms, and to be humored in my attempt to pretend I was actually in charge.

Because our plans to leave Bargaun before dark were foiled by this unexpected event, we decided it would be best to get some rest and leave at three in the morning to catch our 6 a.m. flight out of Simikot. I was beyond fatigued and had hoped to be able to sleep for a few hours, but trying to assimilate all that occurred was too much for my mind to process, and I stayed awake trying to put all the pieces together. To this day, what happened that night never quite managed to form any kind of concrete whole. It was one thing to observe others channeling beings through them, and quite another to be used as a medium myself. The ordeal is now sequestered in a corner of my psyche and marks an event horizon. My concept of reality and of myself crossed into a black hole from which it could never emerge again the same as it had been. Karel put it best when he said, "I know something happened. I know it was real, but it's so far out of my realm of experience, I'm not quite sure where to put it, so I'm just going to file it for now."

Getting up the following morning, the hangover from what happened the night before was severe, with parts of my memory blacked out, my head feeling like it was being jackhammered, and my body moving as if it were in molasses. I also felt the shame of having been so out of control and unable to apologize away anything I may have said or done in that state. But we had a journey to continue and a mission to fulfill. So I put on my boots, zipped up my shell, and threw my backpack over my shoulder. We found ourselves trekking in the dark once more, this time heading uphill and running toward daybreak.

CHAPTER 9

Medicine Potentization

Ladakh, India
(the Reward/Seizing the Sword)

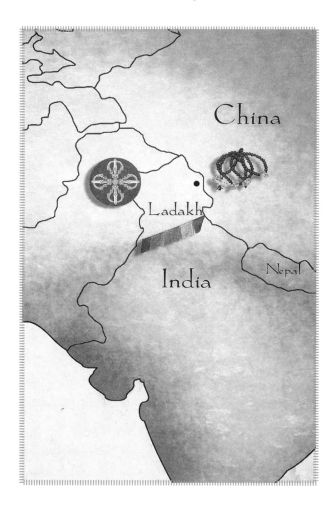

You would've thought we were at the Four Seasons Simikot. The guesthouse had a hot shower in an outdoor stall with a solar-heated water bag, actual beds made of wood frames with thin mattresses, and laundry service provided by one of the staff scrubbing it all by hand. This was the lap of luxury compared to what we'd been used to during our trek through Humla, and we were so appreciative of these amenities of comfort. I had proposed that we draw straws to see who would get to take a shower first because it could take hours for the one bag to keep reheating enough water for all of us to get clean, but I was overruled with a unanimous decision that it should be me. This was not because I was the director, nor because I was somehow more privileged. It was because I was the one who smelled the worst. Apparently, during my ordeal, I had been blessed many times with sacred yak butter rubbed into my clothing and my hair. Within a twenty-four-hour cycle, it seems, yak butter on a trekking body actually turns rancid and is quite fragrant—think soured milk blended with a musky goat. So, as much as everyone else was dying to take a hot shower, the desire to no longer smell the stench coming from me took precedence.

We'd made it to Simikot with plenty of time to spare before our plane was due to arrive to take us back to Nepalgung, then to Kathmandu. But due to strong winds, the pilot never arrived in Simikot and wasn't planning to come until he felt it was safe enough to fly. "It could be two days, four days, or maybe even a week," one of the locals told us. They said this was due not only to the weather but also to the fact that this particular pilot was rather fickle. That's how we ended up at the guesthouse in Simikot with time to kill and a chance to catch our breath.

Although we'd previously been eager to move onto our next location, after our eventful day in Bargaun, we were all grateful for the break. And if

we hadn't had this time, we never would have had the chance to invite ourselves to Thomas's next adventure. If things had proceeded as planned, we
would have continued to our next scheduled destinations—Vietnam and
China—while Thomas went to attend a Tibetan medicine potentization
ceremony in Ladakh, India. Had we parted ways as intended, it might have
been easier just to say our quick good-byes and move on. But having time
to linger in Simikot, and realizing how close we'd all become to Thomas,
it made the thought of abruptly breaking up the band incredibly painful
for Joseph, Karel, Cora, and me. So, we asked if it would be possible for
us to tag along and capture this rare and endangered tradition in which
Tibetan monks and doctors chant mantras over medicine for seven days
and seven nights, infusing it with greater potency.

Even though there was no way for Thomas to ask the head lama in
Ladakh in advance if he could bring guests with video cameras, we took a
leap of faith and decided it would be worth the effort to get visas, change
our airline tickets, and risk being turned away. Cora and Thomas would
have to make calls from the one phone in Simikot that was only available
for a couple hours midday to try to book last-minute flights to India for
five of us, and to plead with the Indian embassy in Nepal to give us travel
visas within a twenty-four-hour turnaround. If we succeeded, we would
be the first people ever allowed to capture on film or video this unique
tradition we hadn't even known existed.

We couldn't decide which was worse, the Hindi electropop music blaring
from the rooftop next door or the deafening whirring of the air condi-
tioner in our eight- by six-foot hotel room. Because it was unbearably hot
in Delhi, especially after just having been in the cool mountains of Nepal,
Cora and I had to decide between opening the window and subjecting
ourselves to our neighbors' partying or shutting ourselves in with the cooling unit that sounded like a garbage disposal. We opted for the former and
were amazed to find that our fatigue took over and kept us asleep until
our alarm went off at 4 a.m. Although I didn't relish having to get up so
early, and we'd only been in Delhi for seven hours, I couldn't wait to leave

its heat, crowded streets, and frenetic energy to make our way north to the mountains of Ladakh. Now part of India's northernmost tip, Ladakh was once ruled by Tibetan royalty and is sometimes still referred to as Little Tibet. While Ladakhis embrace their Tibetan heritage, they are also very proud to have their own unique culture and language.

We fled Delhi, flew over the sharp snow-covered peaks of the Indian Himalayas, and landed in Leh to clear skies, twenty-six degrees Fahrenheit, and crisp dry air at 11,500 feet. At the airport, Dorje, our host from the Jigmet Guest House, warmly greeted us and took us through the town of Leh, which was once the capital and remains the largest town in Ladakh. We were scheduled to spend one night there, and then drive south to the remote village of Chang Tang Nyee, where the medicine potentization ceremony traditionally takes place annually.

The guesthouse was clean and quaint, and the hospitality made us feel as if we were truly guests in someone's home rather than staying in a hotel. I'm sure it helped that Dorje had history with Thomas, who had passed through here many times on past trips to Ladakh. From our spacious rooms we could see the ancient fortress on the mountain above and hear the rushing stream below. Because Leh was a key stop on ancient trade routes between Tibet and Kashmir, we could hear evidence of Leh's history of religious tolerance: Tibetan horns, drums, and chanting filled the air, and the Muslim call to prayer boomed over loudspeakers five times a day.

I was still feeling wobbly from my experience in Nepal, so having a bit more furlough from putting on my director's hat again was a gift. As I stood on the balcony warming my bones in the sun, I watched the donkey that had just been born to the guesthouse family two days prior. It was wobbly, too, testing the novel experience of physical form and getting accustomed to frolicking on brand-new legs. After a bit of running around with its mother nearby, it fell into a pit and couldn't get out. The braying as he and his mother cried for help was nearly unbearable while I stood by unable to help. It took some time for Dorje to find some friends to lift the little one out, but once they did, it was a relief and triumph for all of us. It also seemed a sign of hope that I, too, could be uplifted, pulled from the darkness of fear and confusion from what had happened to me.

After a restful night at the guesthouse, we prepared for a half-day's drive to Chang Tang Nyee, or Nyee for short. As our drivers loaded our gear into two old Land Rovers, we were approached by a group of townswomen who were all dressed up in their traditional Ladakhi costumes—wool robes, colorful quilted top hats with brims on the side that looked like wings, and jewelry made of gold, turquoise, and coral. We were deeply touched that they would come to see us off. There wasn't much fanfare, as the women were shy, but they stood there, beaming with smiles, and giggled when Thomas asked if he could take their photo.

As we drove on narrow rough roads, we were surrounded by the barren scenery of Ladakh heading into winter—a moonscape of rock, gravel, and dirt painted with hues of gray, gold, red, and purple. The turquoise green of the Indus River was our companion, snaking at our side most of the way. In the late morning, we came upon a valley that had a sea of ancient chortens—hundreds of shrines built to honor the Buddha and high lamas. In the sixteenth century, the King of Shey commissioned the chortens to be built by prisoners so they could transform their crimes into merit. The sacred whitewashed structures—each originally constructed with a square base supporting a stair-step pyramid that then came to a bulbous peak—were in various states from centuries of erosion by the elements. Some retained a semblance of their original shape and design, while others were reduced to mere mounds of stone and mud. The chortens varied in size, like grave markers at a cemetery might range from headstones to mausoleums. We walked among them, and they felt at once like dying relics and living tributes to those who had come for hundreds of years to worship in their midst.

Tension was in the air when we arrived in Nyee for several reasons. First, our drivers decided they would double the price they'd quoted us to get us there and back to Leh, and threatened not to come back for us if we didn't agree. Second, because there are no paid accommodations in the village, the host family was at a loss for what to do. They had only planned to have one guest in their home, not five people of mixed genders with a lot of gear and luggage. Lastly, the villagers were concerned that because we'd come unannounced, the leader of the medicine potentization ceremony, Lama Rigzin, may have an objection to opening what Thomas referred to as "a sealed mandala" to strangers. They had to figure out the proper protocol for giving a warm welcome to the invited guest while possibly having to ask his companions to leave. It was an awkward moment for which I felt shamefully responsible.

We resolved the transportation issue by agreeing to the drivers' new price, but only giving them half of that amount, with the other half payable when they came back for us. Dawa, the community leader, head of the host family and son of one of the lead amchis, generously offered us his family's great room—the one that gets the most sun and therefore is the warmest and the most prized—to store our gear and for all of us to sleep in. They also offered the use of a smaller room as a kitchen. The house was a single-story stone-and-mud structure with a total of five rooms, so their giving us two of them was incredibly generous. Dawa decided that whether we were granted permission to attend the ceremony or not, he would allow us at least to be welcomed in his home for the duration of the seven-day ritual. And the villagers arranged for us to have a private meeting with Lama Rigzin to make our case as to why he should allow us not only to attend the ceremony but to also bring in our cameras. It was agreed that the villagers would support whatever he decided and we would comply accordingly.

During our meeting with Lama Rigzin, we all sat in a circle in Dawa's great room. Our liaison and translator, Amchi Tsewang Smanla, a doctor from another village and active in the preservation of Tibetan medicine in all of Ladakh, spoke English, Tibetan, and Ladakhi. He also founded the Yuthog Foundation of Tibetan Medicine, a center for training practitioners in Tibetan medicine. Amchi Smanla presented our case to Lama Rigzin, explaining that we were making a documentary on various healing and spiritual traditions in hopes of preserving them. Lama Rigzin listened intently before he spoke. When he did, he smiled and kindly expressed respect for what we were attempting to do, but like Tsering in Humla, he had doubts that we could fully represent the depth, sacredness, and significance of the medicine potentization ceremony. He shook his head and was just about to decline our request when I blurted out to Amchi Smanla, "May I speak?" Once again, it was a tense, awkward moment because when anyone interrupts a head lama while he's speaking, let alone a stranger, it could be taken as a sign of grave disrespect. I knew I was taking a big risk, but felt compelled to make my case.

I asked Amchi Smanla if he would tell Lama Rigzin that we did understand his concerns and that he was correct in his assessment that we would only be presenting a small slice of the vastness of his tradition. But our hope was to be able to catalyze our viewers to want to learn more about the ceremony and the Tibetan medicine practices as well as capture some of the healing transmissions evoked during the ceremony to spread to others around the world. Following my plea, there followed what seemed an interminable silence while he pondered what I had said. When he had given it enough concentrated thought, he replied, "It seems we have karma together, as you have come unexpectedly from so far away for our paths to cross here. Because we share the same intention of educating and spreading healing to as many as possible, and I can see your heart, all doors are open to you. I will make myself, the lamas, and the amchis available to you for any questions you may have."

A collective exhale could be heard, and then we all grinned, knowing the significance of this moment for us and for the amchis. Of course, it could also have been because all of us in the LBC had been holding our breath and then had to try to recover it at 12,500 feet. Lama Rigzin knew full well that his tradition was in danger of extinction due to modernization and environmental, economical, and political factors, all of which were contributing to a shortage of medicinal herbs, available students, and formal education for the mastery of Tibetan medicine, which can take over a decade. In the following years, they considered that they may have to reduce their seven-day ceremony to three because it was such a hardship on the participants to find the means to travel long distances to Nyee and to be away from their farms and jobs for so long. It was an honor that he saw us as being on the same team. I put my hands in prayer over my heart and said "Thank you" in Ladakhi. Note to any would-be world travelers:

always learn how to say "thank you" first in the language of the places you are visiting, even before "hello." Showing gratitude is the biggest icebreaker and door opener. Luckily in Ladakhi, the same word, *jule* (pronounced joo-lay), covers "hello," "good-bye," and "thank you."

There's something quite extraordinary about watching a bunch of powerful men delicately making beautiful cakes. Some of the *tormas,* or offering cakes, would be presented to the altar of the Medicine Buddha, some distributed among the ceremony participants and nomadic patients who would come to receive treatments, and others would be scattered in the wind to encourage helpful deities to come forth and discourage lesser spirits from causing trouble. While Lama Rigzin, along with the other lamas and amchis, rhythmically mixed the dough, meticulously shaped the cakes, and carefully topped the tormas with exquisite dyed butter sculptures, he taught us the significance of making the tormas as the first step in the medicine potentization ceremony.

"Tormas come in many shapes, colors, and sizes to represent the many forms of creation," Lama Rigzin began. "The syllable *tor* means to scatter, spread, or give away without attachment. *Ma* has connotations of the mother and her representing all sentient beings. So, *torma* signifies the spreading of harmony, wealth, peace, and healing to all sentient beings, with generosity and compassion."

When I asked him what he was working on, he replied, "Today, I am making three particular tormas, and they represent the guru (teacher), which in this case is the Medicine Buddha; the *yidam* (protective deity); and the *khandro* (a goddess—she who moves through space, the sky dancer). And when I make the tormas, I meditate on the guru, the protector, and the goddess so that the tormas transform into each of them." He went on to explain that the tormas begin as base elements of toasted barley flour, butter, milk, and sugar, but once those elements are transformed into a torma, they are sanctified and become a sacramental substance—a nectar for spiritual and physical well-being. This is just like the medicine, which begins as the base elements of plants, minerals, and other ingredients and

must be formulated with clear intention and precision, and then sanctified through a potentization process of prayer, chanting, and meditation
to become a powerful effective remedy against illness.

Lama Rigzin commented on how the concept of tending to both the
divine and the secular was the reason most amchis were also lamas, and
why the Tibetans traditionally did not separate religion and government.
Because healing is seen as a sacred practice to help mind (which includes
spirit) and body, it is natural for a doctor to also be learned in the spiritual
teachings of a monk. The dual training gives the practitioner a greater
context for easing disease and illness on multiple levels. And in regard to a
collective, Lama Rigzin added that religious practice is there to help us better our minds, whereas governance is necessary to help protect the physical
needs and manage the worldly activities of the populace. Therefore, in the
individual or in a group, the two aspects of mind and physical form must
both be cared for in tandem.

Lama Rigzin, whose father was a lama, amchi, and monastery teacher,
began his studies as a monk reading and reciting prayers when he was eight
years old, passing his exams at age fourteen. He then deepened his spiritual
training by going to Tibet and studying the Six Dharmas of Naropa—an
advanced set of practices meant to accelerate the attainment of spiritual
empowerments (sometimes referred to as supernatural powers) and enlightenment. Although Lama Rigzin became adept at these spiritual practices,
his teacher, Apho Rinpoche, a well-respected yogi and enlightened master,
insisted that Lama Rigzin continue his family lineage and study medicine
as well. The training of a doctor of Tibetan medicine is rigorous and similar
to a doctorate program in the West, taking an average of ten years from
start to finish and potentially lasting up to twenty years. "I chose to be a
doctor because I realized that the most precious life of all is human life,"
Lama Rigzin explained. "The reason it is precious is because humans have
the ability to become enlightened, to exchange, and to communicate. Saving a precious human life means that I am engaging in the most sublime
generosity because saving the lives of others is the greatest gift."

When the tormas were complete, we followed the amchis and lamas as
they mindfully walked in slow procession over rocky terrain, ditches, and

icy patches, carefully carrying their trays of precious cargo from the torma room to the monastery. This was part of the second step of the ceremony: the preparation of the altar. In addition to the tormas, raw medicinal herbs, prepared medicine in the form of pills or powders, and medical instruments were also brought to the monastery. The attending amchis, who had come from throughout Ladakh, brought bags of medicine from their home villages to be blessed and empowered, as well as to exchange with other amchis for what they did not have access to in their own areas. A sampling of all the offering items were put on the altar in front of statues of the Medicine Buddha and of Yuthog, the eighth-century Tibetan doctor, monk, and scholar known as the father of Tibetan medicine, who established the first Tibetan medical school and integrated the Indian, Chinese, and Tibetan medical traditions of the time.

They made it look so easy. Hold bowl, add a little warm yak butter tea, grab some toasted barley flour and place in bowl, roll it all together with fingertips, pick up *tsampa* ball, and eat it. Then wash down with soup. The amchis and lamas had invited us to join them for lunch outside the monastery courtyard. We were all seated in a circle, and while they and the other LBC members were deftly making these dough balls, eating, talking, laughing, and enjoying the fresh air and warm sun, there I was completely flummoxed by having to roll my own. For some reason, I just could not get it to the right consistency. It would either be too wet to pick up or so dry that it would fall apart before reaching my mouth. With my repeated attempts to get it right by adding liquid and flour to my bowl, I could have had the record for biggest tsampa ball ever seen in Ladakh, if only I could get it to be a cohesive mass. Now, I thought I was having an inner struggle and would figure it out eventually, but when I looked up I realized everyone was looking at me. They actually had to ask the cook to help me for fear that I would starve. My teammates laughed, but I think it was in that moment that the locals decided I was the slow one in the group, and they had extra compassion for me in whatever I did in the village. I guess it didn't help that the day before the tsampa fiasco, when I thought no one was looking, I was actually talking to a yak, kissed it on the head, and let it lick my hand. I'd experienced the same looks of compassion then—the kind reserved for people you might feel a little sorry for.

Later on, when I was trying to accept the local custom of no paper products while I and the rest of the crew were suffering from the flu, I believe the powers-that-be were once again keeping an eye on their not-quite-right guest. Because the temperatures were so cold, there was only a small stream as a source of water; it was mostly frozen but trickled during the middle of the day. I had seen a spot near the stream where the women did their laundry. Because I had one cloth handkerchief, it needed to be washed as often as possible. So I'd planned to wash it as soon as the stream was running and again before it was about to freeze in the afternoon. The good news about being at such a cold, windy place at high altitude is that laundered things placed in the sun can dry in less than an hour, though some can get so hard they break if not warmed properly indoors.

As I started to do my laundry, Dawa's wife, Thinles Angmo, ran toward me, saying in a high-pitched urgency, "No, no, no, no, no!" and then ran off. I didn't understand and thought I must have done something to offend her. Perhaps there were rules around the use of the stream that I wasn't aware of. I looked down at my hands, chafed from the freezing water and wind, and didn't know what to do, so I just sat there looking like … well, the village idiot. About half an hour later, Thinles Angmo came back with a bucket of steaming water. She poured it into my wash pan and said, "Hot! Not cold!" and walked away. This means that in that time, she had to collect wood, use her precious collected water, heat it, then carry it all the way from her kitchen to the stream's edge in order to teach me how to do laundry properly. Several times in my life I'd been accused of feigning incompetence so that others would help me with things I didn't like to do, but there was no pretending here. I truly was neither capable nor savvy enough to survive in a harsh place like Nyee without the soft hearts of its people.

The chanting had begun. The third stage of the medicine potentization ceremony was the purification process. The space, participants, and ritual objects all had to be cleansed of any negative energy and purified before the potentization could take place. The amchis and lamas had gathered in the monastery and unwrapped from folded cloth their prayer books, which were rectangular loose pages about eleven inches long and three inches high, and inscribed with mantras. Along with the chanting, cymbals, horns, and drums also filled the air in a complex composition of what Scott, one of our film editors, while reviewing the footage later, would refer to as the sounds of Tibetan free jazz.

The lamas and amchis were seated on the floor behind foot-high tables that stretched along three walls of the monastery, while two assistants stood in front of the room at the fourth wall, which housed the altar. One of the assistants was a lama-in-training who was so handsome and photogenic—with his high cheekbones and gleaming white teeth—that the crew and I nicknamed him Hollywood. The other assistant was a rarity—a woman who was introduced to us as *ani,* a title of respect that means "nun." Most of these ceremonies are usually only done and run by men, but Ani's husband, who passed away but had been an integral part of this gathering, used to rely on her to organize the people, care for the ritual objects, and keep everyone on task during this special event. So, she was extremely qualified, well respected, and welcomed by all the participants. Thomas let us know later that because Ani was already an exception, it was also an unusual and precious honor that Cora and I had been invited into the mandala (sacred circle).

Ani lit butter lamps, incense sticks, and in a large metal pot, dried juniper branches. While Hollywood wafted the incense and waved prayer flags in front of the altar to clear it, Ani circled the room with the smoking juniper pot. She stopped before each of us, and we used our hands to direct the fragrant billow over our heads and heart so that we, too, could be cleansed. Then Amchi Paljor, one of the lead amchis, lifted a *phurba*—a three-sided ritual dagger that looked like a fancy tent stake—and stabbed it into a sacrificial torma as an act symbolic of slicing through negativity and vanquishing destructive forces. Ani then tossed the crumbled cake outside over the balcony of the monastery. For the last part of the purification process, Lama Rigzin poured *amrit* (sacred nectar) from a tall antique copper pot, which looked like it could be used for high tea, onto a mirror as a rite for clearing all obfuscations or distortions.

The purification process rolled right into the actual potentization of the medicine, the fourth phase of the ceremony. Amchi Paljor was handed a *dorje* (a small double-headed scepter) with a delicate rainbow cord that was connected to the Medicine Buddha statue on the altar. A dorje is said to represent the masculine aspects, the power of a thunderbolt, and the clarity and indestructibility of a diamond. With his eyes closed and his kind, round face at peace in deep meditation, Amchi Paljor gracefully moved his hands through a series of mudras (sacred symbolic hand gestures), and then put the dorje to his heart. For seven days and seven nights the dorje would remain in uninterrupted connection between the Medicine Buddha and the heart of one of the amchis.

It's amazing how kids always find a way to play with what is available. Just as the amchis and lamas took shifts keeping the ceremony going 24–7, our team members also alternated with each other, with some of us in attendance while the others took breaks to make meals, rest, do laundry, or explore the village. It was on one such break that Cora and I watched a group of kids sliding over ice patches on the barren terrain, in squatting position with wooden boxes tied to their feet. We then walked past piles of mani stones of various sizes inscribed with mantras and greeted some nomadic women passing by.

That afternoon, we also visited with Thinles Angmo as she proudly showed us her small one-room medical clinic at the edge of the village. While her husband was a village leader and the son of a lead amchi, she too was taking a leadership position in the care of her community. The Indian government had trained her as a medical assistant and set up a Western medicine clinic, where people from around the area could come to receive immunizations, birth control, and first-aid care for minor illnesses and injuries. The government program had helped her to learn some basic

English as well. While we were there, some patients arrived on a bus and we witnessed the anguish of a baby who had to endure the pain of getting a shot, while various people throughout the day came to get anything from antibiotics to cold medicine to pain relievers. Thinles said that she believes in integrating both types of medicine because Western medicine is good for immediate cures while Tibetan medicine is good for treating deeper illnesses that take time to heal.

During another break, I realized that because I hadn't been feeling well since the occurrence in Nepal, perhaps I should see one of the amchis. It seemed silly not to ask for help at a gathering of doctors and monks who were trained in treating physical and spiritual illnesses. I understand now that I had a fear that what happened in Nepal might happen again, especially because, aside from the cold that all of us on the crew eventually caught, I'd had some similar symptoms of nausea, light-headedness, and weakness. Of course, all that could also have been due to the illness and the high altitude, but I wanted to be sure.

Amchi Smanla, who had been doing a stellar job of translating and explaining the ceremony to us, arranged for me to meet with the eldest and most venerated lama in the group. Amchi Smanla was surprised and a bit uncomfortable that we'd be sent straight to the top, but it was Lama Rigzin and the other lead amchis who'd decided, considering the type of illness Amchi Smanla had described, that the eldest lama should deal with me.

And then, in the head lama's prayer room, it happened again. I was seated in front of this kind elder, trying to explain to him through Amchi Smanla what had happened in Nepal. Thomas was there and filled in the gaps where I didn't have clear memory. Then that same feeling of losing all strength in my body came over me again, I began to shake, and then I lost track of the details of what happened. I do know that somewhere in me I decided I would not fight it this time. Perhaps that's why it was easier to go through. According to Thomas, I had spoken in tongues again, then spoken in English, but did not weep, scream, or struggle. The episode did not last as long, only about thirty minutes versus several hours, and was not nearly as harrowing. Unlike the previous experience, I felt lighter and less fatigued afterward. Apparently, a message came through me that was meant to be a private one for the amchis, so they all gathered to hear it from Elder Lama and Amchi Smanla. Amchi Smanla was admittedly a little freaked out. He was used to dealing with physical illnesses and was uncomfortable being a part of something so strange, especially from someone he did not know well. The failed tsampa-making attempt and yak-kissing incidents may have also played a part in his questioning my sanity. Luckily, it did not seem as if the lamas and amchis were disturbed by what happened. They were only concerned with how they would execute the instructions of the secret message. Part of the instructions required that the message remain private, and so even now I am not at liberty to share its contents.

The next day, I was called in to see Amchi Paljor, the amchi who was the first to put the dorje to his heart. I learned later that he specialized in the Tibetan mystical healing arts. Amchi Paljor began our conversation by gently asking me how long I'd had this type of illness and how often it had occurred before. Rather than trying to explain the ordeal again, I proposed that he watch the videotapes of what happened in Nepal. Joseph set up the camera to replay the tapes, lent Amchi Paljor his earbuds, and hit *play*. It was the first time I'd seen the videos, and seeing myself say and do things I could not recall was embarrassing, overwhelming, and downright scary. Amchi Paljor, however, was calm and rather nonchalant about the whole thing, which I found immensely comforting.

When Amchi Paljor was done watching the tapes, we had to find a translator, as Amchi Smanla had to leave unexpectedly due to a family emergency. Amchi Paljor conscripted Karma, a translator who was in Nyee working on another project, into service to help us. Karma didn't have much of a choice because as a Tibetan Buddhist, when a high lama and a lead amchi ask for your help, it would be disrespectful to refuse. Through Karma, Amchi Paljor said, "This was not an ordinary possession. It was an oracular occurrence." When this happens, he explained, the person is a channel through which high deities (as opposed to mere ghosts or pesky demons) give advice and prophecy. "We believe a female deity came through you and is Buddhist in origin due to the nature of the messages she gave," he added. Amchi Paljor went on to say that this gift of being a medium could be dangerous if one is not properly trained, and he believed that was why I had such difficulty in Nepal. The Tibetan oracle tradition views this type of channel as a sacred vessel that must be properly prepared and maintained in order to withstand housing these powerful energies. The greatest gift that Amchi Paljor gave me was his perception of both events. They indicated something significant but were completely understandable in the context of his cosmology. He somehow made what happened seem normal, which made me feel saner.

Before we parted, Amchi Paljor handed me his card; on the back he had written the contact information of a Tibetan *rinpoche* (precious jewel, master teacher) in New York to whom he was intimately connected. He suggested that I see this teacher and show him the tapes of the events in Nepal and Nyee. This teacher would not only be able to give me proper training but would also be able to help the amchis and lamas in Ladakh to execute the oracle's message. It dawned on me that I'd been pretty self-absorbed about what the channeling events had meant for me, but Amchi Paljor's last words were another reminder that I was being led down a path that was greater than simply overcoming my personal fears or just making a film.

When we finished, poor Karma was feeling stressed as his supervisor, Laurent Pordié, had been calling for him and wondering where he'd gone. Laurent, a French anthropologist and ethnopharmacologist, was in Ladakh to develop programs for the training of amchis, the preservation of amchi medicine knowledge, and the cultivation of Tibetan medicinal plants. I asked Karma to introduce me to Laurent so I could personally apologize to him and explain why Karma was put in a bit of a bad position. When I met Laurent and learned about what he was doing, I was so impressed that as someone still in his twenties he had already made such headway with his projects. Because we had the common goal of preserving healing traditions around the world—his with on-the-ground initiatives and mine through film—we immediately hit it off, and he was very forgiving of our kidnapping his translator. Laurent's work also gave me great hope that something was already being done to support the amchi way of life.

Being enveloped in love is the best way I can describe what it felt like to sit among the amchis and lamas during those seven days of ceremony. On the last day, we were all in attendance for the fifth stage—the closing. As the clarinet-sounding horns played, and the lamas and amchis chanted, it was bittersweet to know we had been privy to such a special, powerful event, yet would no longer be surrounded by the continuous prayers, earnest intentions, and sounds of compassion.

The amchis and lamas tossed rice to represent the spreading of healing, and then redistributed the bags of medicine that had been housed behind the altar back to the amchis who had brought them. Now infused with greater power and efficacy, the medicine was ready to be disseminated to all the patients the amchis would treat in the year ahead. A bowl of amrit was passed among the amchis, who each added a sample from their medicine bags. Once the bowl made its rounds, Lama Rigzin blessed it, and then one of the amchis ladled a spoonful of the blend in each of our palms. We then ingested the potentiated medicine. Ani walked around the room with a bowl of raw medicine that looked like dried seeds and pods of various sizes. We each took a piece from the bowl. I chose something that was the size of an avocado seed. *Chai* (sweet tea) was poured in small cups for each of us, and sugary snacks and pieces of torma were passed around. After we ate and drank the sweet things symbolic of spiritual nectar, the ceremony was closed with Ani once again coming to each of us with the smoking pot of juniper so that we might leave the ceremony purified. Just as the medicine would be sent out into the world carrying the bounty, benefits, and healing power generated by the amchis, I hoped it would be the same for each of us who were so fortunate to have witnessed this medicine potentization ceremony.

Sure there are differences between Western and Tibetan medicine, but it's like water that comes from different sources but flows to the ocean. All medicine is for the good of humankind and the healing of diseases.

—Lama Rigzin Lamdang
Chang Tang Nyee, Ladakh

CHAPTER 10

Same Same Only Different

Vietnam (the Road Back, Part 1)

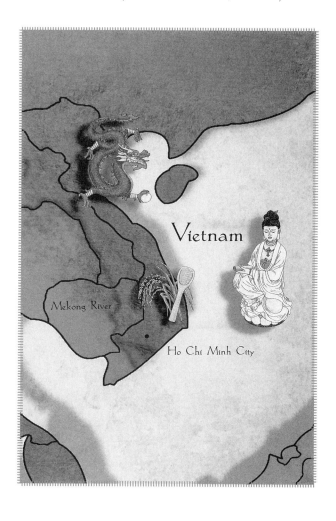

"If you go back looking for our past, you'll only find death and sorrow. Focus on the present and keep your eyes looking forward," my mom cautioned me when she learned I was headed to Vietnam. I would be the first person in my family to return since we'd fled the war in 1968, and my going back filled her with trepidation—an overwhelming fear that something bad would happen to me. The emotional remnants of managing to get her four children safely out of a war-torn country as a single mom were always looming. But I assured her that I was going to Vietnam as part of my documentary project, would be accompanied by my crew the entire time, and was not at all interested in excavating what we'd left behind. But old souvenirs have a way of surfacing despite our efforts at keeping them neatly packed away in the storerooms of our psyches.

Our trip to Vietnam was supposed to be light in terms of film production. It was the one place where the itinerary was left purposely more open and fluid by Cora, who had accurately predetermined that she'd have a road-weary, mind-bleary crew a month into intensive shooting. We only had four things firmly placed on our schedule—meet up with Trinh, our girlfriend from Seattle, who would help us to translate and navigate; visit with neighbors and friends of Aunty Lien, my healer aunt living in San Jose, to learn more about her time as a healer in Saigon (now known as Ho Chi Minh City); visit one of the temples she had directed us to; and take a mini beach vacation. Yep, another perk of membership in the Lucky Bastards Club—designated workcations! After the cold and dry of the Himalayas, Joseph, Karel, Cora, and I were looking forward to exploring the healing properties of a brand-new beachside eco-resort on the shores of Nha Trang. We did have some loose interviews planned with healers in various parts of the country, but it had been hard to lock those down from afar, so we decided just to arrive and see what happens.

Aunty Lien did not take a gondola lift up the mountain when she'd made her pilgrimage to the temple at Núi Bà Den (Black Lady Mountain) before escaping Vietnam in 1990. The open two-person cabled pods the crew and I rode to get to the top were built after the war and were much like a chairlift at a ski area. Aunty Lien had to scale the perilous trails up the 3,200-foot-high mountain as part of her appeal to be released from her healer's tour of duty. The highest point in southern Vietnam and located sixty miles northwest of Ho Chi Minh City, Núi Bà Den jutted up from the surrounding flatlands, bearing many contradictions. It has traditionally been a sacred place for Cambodian and Vietnamese people of various ethnicities and religions, and historically a strategic military post that had seen fierce combat in wartime. It is the site of Buddhist temples and a theme park complete with brightly painted concrete cartoonish animal statues, a train, paddleboats, and a luge slide ride. It houses sacred caves that shelter monks and nuns and old tunnels where armies once stored arms and hid soldiers. It is a dead volcano that is a symbol of life.

When we arrived at the temple level, we saw a beautiful complex with one main shrine and several small altar areas. The temple had been destroyed during the Vietnam-American War, but it had all been rebuilt. There were statues of Quan Am, of the Black Lady deity, and of the many aspects of the Buddha placed around the exterior and the interior of the temple. The main temple building was rectangular and had three levels, each progressively smaller than the previous one with roof corners that curled upward and were decorated with gold mythical animals that looked like dragons. Before going in, I lit some large sticks of incense in the fire pit and said a prayer for my ancestors, for my loved ones, and for all sentient beings, then placed the smoking sticks in a large clay pot of sand at the foot of a large Quan Am statue, standing six feet above me.

The sound of a monk chanting and the rhythmic tapping of his percussive instrument—a stick hitting a wooden block—lured us inside. We removed our shoes and walked into the ornate open-air room, mindful that we were in a place of worship. Because Aunt Lien had sent me here, I seemed to be looking for something or waiting to feel something. Although I was respectful and got on the floor, sat on my heels, and prayed, it was hard for me to feel connected to anything profound looking up at the modern Buddha statue with neon rays emanating flashing rainbow lights from his head. I did, however, appreciate that the postwar communist government would put a significant amount of resources toward rebuilding this religious site. Despite the monk's earnest chanting, banging of the gong, and lighting of incense, I just couldn't drop into any sort of spiritual experience.

We left the temple grounds having shot some nice beauty footage and then headed back to catch the cable chairs down. We came across a tourist who was headed toward us, and he let us in on his great find. He told us to continue past the gondola station and look for Green Dragon Cave. After walking around a bend, we'd follow some stone steps, which would lead us up to a landing with a Quan Am statue pagoda and a small cave opening about six feet high and four feet wide. When we got there, a skinny old monk emerged from the cave and greeted us with a toothless smile. He placed his hands in prayer position before his heart, bowed his head, and invited us in. The cave was maybe forty square feet, its walls lined with altars to Quan Am and the Buddha—some built and some sitting in the natural nooks and crannies of the rock formations. The altars were lit with candles and were adorned with foot-tall statues of various deities. Burning incense filled the space with a gossamer veil. We learned that the monk was the caretaker of the cave and lived only on the alms of visitors. Being in the presence of his devotion and surrounded by the natural setting of the cave, I finally found a sense of peace and well-being. When we stepped outside the cave, a fog rolled in and enveloped us. Just as the guidebooks said could sometimes happen on Black Lady Mountain, we were indeed among the clouds.

Ho Chi Minh City is a bustling, crowded, loud place not unlike many of the large cities in developing countries. Swirls of cars, trucks, mopeds, bicycles, and pedestrians move in ordered chaos along the streets and around the intersections to the ever-present deafening cacophony of beeping horns. As we made our way around the city, it was apparent that despite having a communist government, the spirit of entrepreneurship of the Vietnamese people did not change with the politics. Aside from the state-owned endeavors, there were plenty of little businesses in every alley and along all the streets—tailors, electronics suppliers, and, yes, nail salons. Wherever there was open space on the sidewalks, someone had set up an impromptu business—from recycled tires made into sandals to haircuts to street food. All these things were positive indications of recovery from wartime. Trinh and I marveled at and took pride in the resilience of "our people" to be able to put one foot in front of the other and not look back.

The LBC had cavalierly eaten its way through Hawaii, Peru, Nepal, and India—from coconut water in plastic bags to skewered rodents to steamed *momos* (Tibetan pot stickers). We weren't about to let caution get in the way of continuing our eating expeditions in Vietnam, despite warnings from those in the know for us to avoid street food and establishments not approved by the tourist board. We stopped a man on a bicycle cart who was selling hard-boiled fertilized duck eggs. He broke the eggshell at the top, sprinkled salt and pepper into the hole, and handed one to each of us girls. The boys passed on that one, especially when we got beyond the yolk and showed them the soft, partially formed bird embryo we were about to eat.

We stopped at a crevice-in-the-wall place that only had an awning and a single table and ordered a whole ginger-steamed chicken meal. The cook was incredulous when we were done, and Karel and Joseph asked for another one. Of course, the chickens there were not plumped up on drugs, so it took two to quell the boys' hunger. The double meal cost the equivalent of five dollars. Then there was the incredible goat stew meal, the morning *bánh mì* runs to fetch the Vietnamese sandwiches made with fresh brick-oven baked French baguettes filled with various meats, pickled vegetables, and soy sauce, and the multiple visits to *phở* beef noodle soup) carts. While Cora, Karel, and Joseph enjoyed the culinary adventure, Trinh and I found these familiar tastes of home helped to comfort the underlying discomfort we'd felt since landing in Vietnam.

Despite the economic activity, the friendly greetings, and the good food, there was a nagging feeling that I couldn't quite put my finger on at first. It then began to dawn on me that being *Việt kiều* (Vietnamese living outside Vietnam), Trinh and I weren't treated like the rest of the team by the locals. The Vietnamese citizens did not see us as their compatriots. Instead, we were the defectors. We would learn later that some of the locals even thought we might have been escorts (read: prostitutes) for Karel and Joseph. Trinh said that several times when she'd told people that I, the Vietnamese woman, was the employer of the American men, they didn't believe her. One afternoon, a smiling enthusiastic kid ran alongside us as we walked the streets and asked everyone, proudly using his English skills, "Where you from?" When Joseph and Karel answered, "U.S.," the boy put his thumb up and said, "We love Americans." Cora answered, "Hong Kong," and the boy, pointing back and forth between them, said, "Ah, same same only different," and laughed. When I said, "From here," he looked puzzled and said, "No, you Filipina," and ran off.

It didn't help that my Vietnamese was dreadful, having been replaced by French at the age of four and English at the age of six. When we'd landed at the airport in HCM City, which in my mind will always be Saigon, the customs agent saw my passport and looked at me scornfully. She asked me in Vietnamese if I spoke Vietnamese. I answered "No" in English, not wanting to risk saying something wrong in Vietnamese. She continued in Vietnamese, asking me what I was doing in Vietnam. I continued to answer in English, "Tourist." Because we didn't have any official permits for film production, we'd decided to use our small cameras and just act like tourists. Then she said in English, "Why you no speak Vietnamese?" I answered in Vietnamese, "I can't." She continued to hammer me, "When you leave Vietnam?" I answered in Vietnamese, "When I was so little. I was four years old," and shrugged my shoulders apologetically and looked down like a shamed child. She finally stamped my passport with such force that it sounded like a judge's mallet striking her bench.

⊇

It was such a relief to be back shooting something rather than feeling all the emotions that being in my birthplace stirred up. Having been in Vietnam previously for her art business, Cora secured a driver with a van through her connections. Dong would be our guide and guardian for the rest of our time in Vietnam. A good driver has connections to all the desirable places to stop for whatever you might be seeking and knows all the bad places to avoid, whether to skirt trouble with authorities, to stay clear of bedbugs, or to be safe from food poisoning. We picked up Uncle Sau, Aunty Lien's brother-in-law, and he directed Dong to take us to the old neighborhood where Aunty had lived with her husband and his brother, Uncle Hai. If we were lucky, we could maybe talk to some people who had known her. Not having anything formally planned, and because of our lack-of-permit situation, we were set to do some guerilla shooting, or in layman's terms, catch as catch can.

Uncle Sau spotted a woman he knew, and we all jumped out of the van with cameras loaded and interview mic ready. The poor woman was startled to see this motley crew approaching her, until she recognized Uncle Sau and smiled. He explained what we were doing and she was more than glad to accommodate us. She said, "Oh yes, we miss *Bà* ("lady") very much and wish she would return. Not just because she is a great healer, but because she is such a kind soul." The woman confirmed that there were days when a line of people would form outside Aunty's home and snake all the way around the block. Some of the other neighbors saw what we were doing and gathered around. "Yes, your Aunt helped me with my arthritis, but it's gotten worse since she's left," an older woman chimed in. Yet another woman joined the conversation and said, "Bà never even wanted anything in exchange for her help. But, she did let us give her rice so she could use it as offerings to the goddesses that worked with her." When I asked the women what people would come to Aunt Lien for, they all jumped in at once, forcing Trinh to keep up with all the translations. One said, "I was sick for three years. I was depressed always in a worried state, and people thought I was crazy. I only needed to see Bà once and she cured me." Another said, "When people wanted to know when to escape from Vietnam, she could tell them when it would be safe and which people to trust." Then someone said, "Bà would look completely different when she was healing. Her face changed completely. She would get very stiff and her eyes had no pupils ... they were just white." We weren't sure how we were going to put this all together in a coherent narrative, but we were glad to have met some people with firsthand experience of Aunty Lien's channeled healings and prophecies.

After we dropped off Uncle Sau at his home, we had some free time remaining. Although my memories of Saigon were very different from my experience of Ho Chi Minh City, being with people who knew my aunt, eating familiar foods, and being surrounded by my native language sparked a yearning in me. Against my mother's warning, I'd asked the team and Dong if we could go looking for my childhood home. We drove through busy streets lined with stores, down small alleyways crammed with unmatched homes—some older with fading touches of French colonial architecture, some tall and skinny with the look of modern Chinese construction, sterile with blue and white tiled exteriors—and passed buses, small cars, and pedicabs filled nearly beyond capacity with people. One moped was piled high with an entire family—father driving, mother in the back, one child on the handlebars, another on his father's lap, and a baby in the mother's arms. It was like looking for a needle in a sea of haystacks. So many buildings had been replaced and streets renamed. I only had an old address. Dong placed phone calls as he drove, trying to find clues. After hours of searching, it got dark, and we finally decided to give up. I tried to hide my disappointment, but everyone knew that this had meant more to me than probably anything else on this visit to Vietnam.

The next day, the weight of being in my homeland but not finding home hit me. I had a migraine and didn't want to get out of bed. Trinh came in to check on me. As a torrential downpour began, with flooding and gale-force winds wreaking havoc all up and down this long country, the waterworks sprung from me, too. It turned out that Trinh was having a lot of emotions that she had been keeping at bay as well. She left Vietnam when she was sixteen years old, so she had more memories and must have felt a greater grief than I did. But she never belittled my pain, and in the privacy of my hotel room, we wept together that entire morning.

We understood that while Cora, Karel, and Joseph were looking at the new Vietnam with the eyes of visitors, we saw ghosts of the old Vietnam through the lens of loss. In our weeping we expressed the emotions of being home, but feeling like strangers; of being seen as those who'd fled the burning building while leaving so many behind to rebuild from the ashes; and of feeling so lucky to be healthy and whole while feeling guilty that our good fortune was not shared by all who had suffered. We finally had to admit that being in Vietnam wasn't just about being on a film shoot or on holiday; it was about being surrounded by the familiar, yet accepting that everything we once knew had completely changed.

This was another moment that my mom's *what is bad is good* philosophy came in handy, along with the Buddhist concept of impermanence. After our good cry there was a sort of clarity. Yes, everything had changed, but it needed to. After all, Trinh and I were born into war, lived our early lives in fear, fled the war, and now there was peace. The young people we met said they didn't even care about the war because they didn't remember it. The older people had been focused on rebuilding and forgiving. Life had moved on, and Trinh and I needed to collect the parts of us that were locked in a time capsule and release them into the present. Cora, Karel, and Joseph came to get us. It was time to hit the road. We were headed north.

Slosh, slosh, squish, squish. Our feet were constantly wet after the rains came. Even when we were in the van, our sandals never dried, and each time we stepped out there was no getting around the water because it seemed the entire country was one giant puddle. There was no point in wearing closed-toe shoes, either, for that would only have added another layer of moisture retention. I was reminded of the stories I'd heard of how miserable it was for the American soldiers to have to wear wet combat boots days, weeks, or months at a time during the rainy season. As Dong drove through the storm, he worried that we'd be upset that everything took longer than normal. The usual eight-hour drive from HCM City to Nha Trang ended up taking almost twice as long. We joked that we understood that acts of God are not covered under his Good Guide Guarantee.

We were impressed, however, at Dong's ability to maneuver around pot-holes, washed-out roads, standing water, and rushing floodwaters. Along the way, we passed shrimp farms with their miles of sectioned-off square fields of water overflowing, a man plowing through his flooded fields with a pair of weary oxen, and a bus crossing through several feet of standing water with quacking ducks tied to its roof. Needing a break, we'd stopped at a roadside monastery, whose peacefulness and Quan Am statue were reflected in the stillness of the pool that now engulfed its grounds. A monk opened the doors, pushing them through the water that was as high inside as it was outside, and beckoned us in. Dong stayed with the van while Joseph, Karel, Cora, Trinh, and I rolled up our pants. As the monk came toward us and we went toward him, we all waded into the courtyard through the knee-high puddle making soft ripples, which seemed to radiate his smile in the face of this adversity. I later learned that this was the worst flooding Vietnam had had in sixty years.

As silly as it sounds, we actually went to our eco-resort in Nha Trang at least to check in so we wouldn't be considered no-shows. And I suppose we were holding onto the dream that the winds would blow away the clouds, the floods would recede, and we'd get our much-needed beach break. When we arrived, we were greeted kindly, but told the resort was closed and the guests had been evacuated. But being proud of their new place, the managers gave us a tour, despite the fact that the grounds and many of the buildings were submerged in a foot of water. As daylight was fading, we sloshed around and were able to appreciate the resort's layout, its proximity to the beach, and the architecture of the made-to-look-rustic modern hut accommodations. We couldn't spend too much time feeling sorry for ourselves, as we felt worse for the people whose enthusiasm and hopes for the new place had been dashed by the inclement weather. We'd only missed out on a few days of R&R, but an entire staff's livelihood was at stake, as well as the boost this place could be to the local economy.

Our relaxation plans were not the only things that were foiled. Efforts to contact local healers went nowhere as the weather also caused phone lines to be down, power outages to occur, and people to be evacuated. Trinh had some family who lived in Nha Trang, and her cousin, Anh, braved riding through the floodwaters on a moped to meet us and to help us in any way she could. We managed to find an open hotel in town that still had power and two rooms available. Antsy to shoot something, we saw a man on the street carrying a briefcase and offering cupping treatments, so we asked if he'd be interested in demonstrating his work for our cameras. He seemed as excited as we were to be able to practice his craft, rather than just waiting around for the weather to change.

We decided that the natural choice for the patient should be Dong. He had been a true road warrior for us and had shoulder pain, a sore back, and exhaustion to show for it. The cupping man opened his briefcase and revealed the tools of his trade—about twenty small glass cups that looked like clear round light bulbs, a wire handle, cotton, rubbing alcohol, liniment oil, and a lighter. Dong took off his shirt and lay facedown on the bed while the cupping man put the cotton around the tip of the wire handle, poured alcohol in a bowl, swished the cotton in it, and lit the cotton on fire. He then quickly used the flame to heat a cup before placing it on Dong's back. The heat of the cup created suction against Dong's skin. This was done several times until Dong's entire back was filled with cups stuck to it. As time passed, Dong's skin was drawn further and further into the cups. The cups were left on his back for about fifteen minutes, until the cupping man determined that all the evil wind of illness had been sucked out.

The cupping man removed the cups one by one, revealing welts of pink, red, or purple that remained on Dong's skin where each cup had been. The cupping man explained, "See, the dark purple or deep red ones indicate the places where he had the most pain." The cupping man then rubbed oil all over Dong's back and gave him a little massage to close the healing session. The welts made Dong's back look like a Twister game mat, but with red and purple round spots. They seemed as if they would be extremely painful and made Dong look like he'd been severely burned. Dong, however, said he could feel where the cups had been, but that he was in no pain at all. The cupping man added that although they may look really bad, and it was hard to believe, the marks would disappear completely in about three days. When Dong sat up, he smiled and said,

"I feel much better: less sore, more relaxed. Thank you." Joseph decided that he'd like to try the treatment. Now, I thought the welts looked really bad on Dong, but against Joseph's pale white skin, they looked hideous. Yet, as promised, even Joseph's did indeed fade after a few days.

Because I still had remnants of the cold we'd all caught in Ladakh and wanted something else for us to shoot, Anh offered to do *cao gió* (scrape wind treatment), which was similar to the cupping treatment in its intention of releasing evil wind and increasing blood circulation. Although these two treatments have strict protocols and require serious training in traditional Chinese medicine, in Vietnam they are usually practiced as part of folk medicine. Anh used the same type of menthol-based medicinal oil as the cupping man and rubbed it all over my back. Then she took a silver coin and scratched my back forcefully, and with quick strokes, first up along the spine, then out along the ribs, and across my lower back. My mom actually used to do this to my siblings and me to treat our colds. When we flinched or complained about the pain, she'd say, "The bigger the marks, the stronger the medicine." This treatment leaves horrific-looking scrape marks that can appear like lashes from a whip or bruising, but like the cupping welts, they disappear within two to four days. Anh finished by giving me a light massage and then cocooning me in a sheet. It felt nice to be cared for and nurtured, and I did feel less congested and much better afterward, and not just because the scraping had stopped.

The next day, as we watched people trying to cross a road that had become a raging river, we realized it was time to let go and stop trying to make things happen. The flooding was so bad that some resourceful people improvised and started businesses of ferrying people, animals, mopeds, and bicycles across the road on rafts and boats. A few brave women rolled up their pants and waded across the quick-running waters, which rose to their thighs, with their load of goods or pushing their bicycle. They moved past a bus that had been overturned by the force of the water and just kept moving. One woman was struggling to lead a cow across the rapids, but it was frightened and stopped midway—the most dangerous spot—refusing to budge. I took these vignettes as signs to surrender my expectations, accept that there was no more to be done here, and forge ahead. I guess having my skin scraped with a metal object over and over again pretty much summed up my feelings about returning home. It hurt, but I trusted that somehow it was good medicine and that the marks that appeared to be menacing would fade in no time. As I left Vietnam, I realized that this journey was not so much about going back to find something I'd left behind. It was about having a do-over from having fled in fear, to now walking away with grace, and listening to my mom by keeping my eyes looking forward.

CHAPTER 11

The Blind Seer

Yunnan, China (the Road Back, Part 2)

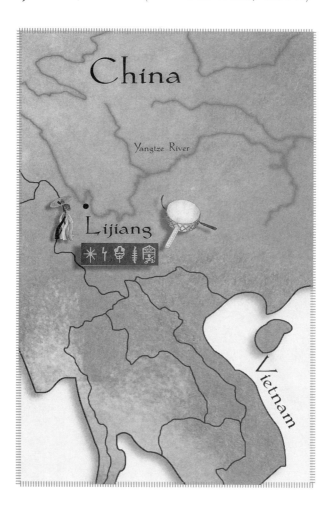

In the old days, a god and a goddess came down from the heavens. They fell in love and chose to stay here together. Once earthbound, they fell ill and had no medicine, so they set out to seek those who might have medicinal and healing knowledge. The god and goddess wandered all over, and their search led them to a dongba—*a well-traveled and learned man of the Naxi people. The dongba had knowledge of both the natural and the spiritual worlds, so he was able to help them.*

There was no written language then, so the wise dongba created a pictograph system to preserve his wisdom. If he saw the sky, he would draw it. If he saw a mountain, he would draw it. He created volumes and volumes of books. But one day, a huge storm came and blew all the dongba's sacred books into the sea. A crab ate the books, and then a giant frog drank all the water in the sea, swallowing the crab and all the texts with it. The knowledge was thought to be lost, but the dongba found the giant frog and was able to reclaim the sacred prayers and wisdom, bringing medicine back to the people.

As the dongba (priest, wise man, shaman) finished the telling of his religion's origination myth, he picked up his octagon-shaped drum and said, "That's why we use this drum and the eight-sided symbol in all our ceremonies. The eight sides represent the eight legs of the crab, and when we beat the drum, we are getting all the prayers back out of the belly of the frog." Then he began the rhythmic drumming and entrancing chanting, and filled the room with blessings and prayers.

Most people think of China as a country that is home to one ethnic group—the Chinese. But, the People's Republic of China recognizes fifty-six different ethnic groups, each with its own unique culture and language, with nearly half of those groups found in Yunnan Province in southwest

China. Although many of these minorities were persecuted during China's Cultural Revolution, now with the increased interest in and profitability of cultural tourism, the Chinese government has created centers that showcase some of these minority groups' traditions. The Naxi is one of those groups, and a Dongba cultural center and museum was established in the town of Lijiang.

Having been introduced to the Naxi culture in her past travels, Cora suggested that our last adventure on this journey for our documentary track the Naxi's Dongba spiritual and healing traditions. Karel and Joseph had left us in Vietnam to head home to spend the holidays with their families. Cora, Trinh, and I made this last leg on our own, flying from Hanoi to Hong Kong, then to Kunming, and landing in Lijiang. Cora continued her role as the producer but also had to step in as the translator. I took the helm behind the camera, while Trinh tagged along offering good company and an extra set of hands to carry gear.

Lijiang is an eight-hundred-year-old town that is close to Tibet in the foothills of the Himalayas, near the Great Bend of the Yangtze River. It was deemed a UNESCO World Heritage Site due to the preservation of its ancient quarters of original centuries-old structures. Lijiang is made up of Old Town, New Old Town, and New Lijiang. The Old Town is where the oldest structures can be found, whereas New Old Town contains new buildings made to look like the original ones. And New Lijiang is the loud, hectic, and generically modern area that was created to accommodate the hordes of tourists.

We got settled in our guesthouse, which was in New Old Town. It had wood-beamed construction, a courtyard, stone and stucco walls, circular doorways, and a tiled roof to mimic the buildings of the Old Town. However, it wasn't hard to see that it was a new flimsy construction when the interior walls in our room had cheap white-and-blue ceramic tiles, some of which had fallen away, and the bathroom had a broken sink faucet and a leaky plastic bathtub. I really couldn't complain too much, keeping in mind that Old Town was not meant to have hotels to house the likes of us, and it was sad to discover that most of the residents who once lived in Old Town had to move away due to the rise in cost of living and to make room for the vendors who moved in to cater to visitors.

After a restful night, the girls and I headed out to find Ben, a Naxi artist who lived in Old Town and had been studying with a dongba. Like many of the other spiritual and healing traditions we'd had a chance to be exposed to, the Dongba tradition was in danger of disappearing due to the discontinuation of father-to-son transmission of the knowledge and the passing of the remaining elderly dongbas. Cora had befriended Ben on a previous trip, and he'd volunteered to be our guide and translator, as he could speak both Naxi and Mandarin. Because no vehicles are allowed in Old Town, stepping into its square was like walking into a bubble of serenity. Or maybe it was just being back near the Himalayas that made me feel more at ease. Although we'd heard the town could get jam-packed with people, we were there on the edge of winter, so we seemed to have the run of the place.

We strolled along the cobblestone walkways, crossing Old Town's many bridges that span the complex of ancient canals that have supplied the town and its residents with fresh river, well, and spring water for hundreds of years. The water was fast moving, crystal clear, and the color of translucent jade. Along one of the canals, a woman was squatting and washing her vegetables. At the edge of another, we saw a black kettle with oil heating over a fire. A woman came out of her home and threw some potato slices into it. Cora discovered that the woman was selling them, and she, Trinh, and I were delighted to dig into the paper bag full of piping-hot potato chips, continuing the LBC food foray tradition. As we neared Ben's art studio, we passed buildings with a look similar to our guesthouse—simple wood-framed structures with plastered white walls, gray tiled roofs, and wooden verandas—and some that were more ornate, with influences from the Ming and Qing dynasties, the styles that any Chinatown area in the United States tries to mimic.

When we arrived at Ben's, he greeted us warmly and invited us to take a tour of his two-story studio. Ben was tall, handsome—with bone structure similar to that of the Tibetans we'd met—and wore a North Face shell and a baseball cap. He was young—maybe in his mid-twenties—yet clearly very successful selling his art to tourists. While we visited, he had his cook make us a *congee* (rice porridge) breakfast. Being three Asian girls, Cora, Trinh, and I loved having this comfort food, which could be made sweet or savory depending on what condiments we added to it. Ben showed us a collection of his beautiful gouache on rice paper paintings that represented Naxi life and incorporated some of the ancient Dongba pictographs. The complex pictograph system, with over one thousand different characters, has been used for centuries to record the history and culture of the Naxi people. Only a dongba can write in the pictograph system and read the ancient texts that are written on wood or specially crafted paper made by a dongba. In talking with Ben, we learned that he was studying with a dongba, not to become one but to find a way to preserve his culture through his art, very much as Don Pablo had done in Peru.

"They've got him on display like he's an animal in a zoo," I protested, then declared resolutely, "I'm not going to participate in this type of exploitation. We're not shooting the dongba." Ben had arranged for us to meet his dongba teacher, but I was conflicted about the circumstances under which I would be allowed to see him. When I heard that we would be visiting the dongba in a cultural center, I really didn't understand what it meant. We had to purchase tickets to get in, walk through a turnstile, and visit a public exhibit that actually contained the dongba's home.

The Dongba cultural center was in an area called Jade Water Village. Ben, Cora, Trinh, and I walked by the beautiful lake that lived up to its name and took the tour by following the map and signs. The village comprised old traditional Naxi buildings, which were simple gray log cabins with wood beams, porches, dirt floors, and pictograph symbols over the doorways. Tourists were allowed to enter the uninhabited homes, look around, and take photos. We then went into the small museum, which had some historical information on the Dongba religion and some of the pictograph religious texts under glass. We learned that the Dongba religion is thought to be over a thousand years old and was influenced by Tibetan and Han cultures. There is still some debate, but some anthropologists believe the Dongba tradition is related to the Tibetan Bon religion, which predates Tibetan Buddhism.

We walked along the stone and gravel pathways and crossed over canals on wooden bridges and appreciated the charm of the village. When we walked farther to the back of the cultural center where people actually lived, we saw some people working in a communal garden in front of their cabins. Then Ben pointed to the home of the dongba, which was marked with pictographs lining the doorway, a wooden triangle above it, and two masks on either side—an orange tiger and a gray yak. I had taken the camera out to get a panoramic shot of the grounds, but it was only then that I realized the entire area was enclosed within a rock wall. Which is when it hit me that this wasn't a demonstration of Naxi culture, but an encasement of it. I felt sick to my stomach and put my camera away. My impulse was to run out of there as quickly as possible, but then the dongba came out of his cabin and greeted Ben and invited us in.

"During the Cultural Revolution, I was sent to a labor camp, and my books were confiscated," the dongba said as we sat in his cabin drinking tea while he smoked a cigarette. He was not wearing his traditional Naxi clothing, but rather some regulation dark green pants and matching wool shirt that fit like pajamas, and a gray driving cap. "My sacred texts are now on display in the museum. You can see them there," he continued. Listening to this gentle elder, I was getting more and more incensed for him. I expressed my feelings about the exploitation and how I had planned to videotape him, but that I now refused to in protest of what the Chinese government was doing to him. He smiled and said, "Well, I can't see my texts anyway because I've been blind since I was a child. I know them all by memory, so I don't need them." He then asked me if I would record him doing some ceremonies and rituals so that I may share his traditions with others who may never be able to come to see him or know of his culture. Although I had perceived him to be in captivity, he told me he saw himself as free because he was now able to practice his religion and teach about it to others. In light of his perception of his own situation, I gladly pulled out my camcorder, and Cora, her still camera.

"My Dongba heritage goes back four generations. I began to study when I was seven years old and was initiated when I was sixteen," he began. "When my grandfather was eighty-five, he began to teach me to be a dongba. I knew everything right away. It was as if I knew it from before. Even though I couldn't read the texts, I seemed to know what was in them." The dongba also explained why he believed he was blind. "In my past life, I was a Buddhist lama. My house caught on fire and I ran back in to get my sacred texts. I did not make it out alive. That's why I cannot see my scriptures in this lifetime." As a dongba, he has knowledge of weather, prophecy, shamanism, and medicine. It is his duty to work at keeping the balance between the human, natural, and spiritual worlds. "To be a dongba you have to be good to everyone and help the health of the people like a doctor," he added.

The dongba then offered to do a sampling of various rituals—a sort of medley of his greatest hits. He said because he is blind, he can't do all the things that the other dongbas can do, like dancing, but that he could still do many things. Donning his traditional robe—a cream linen smock with blue trim and belt-tie that fastened at his right hip—over some pants, the dongba commented on the difference in clothing of a Naxi dongba and a Tibetan lama. "When the Buddhist monks and the dongbas went to the west to seek the sacred scriptures, the dongbas won the race and got the pants. This is why Tibetan Buddhist monks only wear robes, while we dongbas wear robes and pants." He chuckled. For his first three numbers, the dongba wore only a black scarf tied with a topknot on his head. He belted out a melodious chant accompanying himself with a wooden staff that had jingling bells attached to it. Then he played a ram's horn, making a loud sustained warbling sound blowing through the tip and shaking his hand over its bell. He closed this part of the demonstration by moving to a large octagonal drum hanging on the wall and beating it rhythmically, then chanting along. I was surprised to find that the drumming and chanting seemed similar to the rhythm and sounds I'd heard at Native American ceremonies.

When it was time to do the protection ritual, the dongba replaced his headscarf with an ornate headdress—a colorful crown with five prongs depicting five different deities and two round lobes that made him appear as if he had huge ears. He deftly moved around a blazing fire that was in an open pit in one corner of his living area and began a different chant, this one more rapid and urgent in its expression. Although watching the blind dongba, I was concerned about his safety, he had no problem maneuvering so quickly and feeling his way to fetch various things from the shelves, placing them on the floor next to the fire, chanting all the while. He then sat down before the fire and clanged some cymbals connected by a single string. After setting them down, he threw pinches of different things into the fire, causing its flames to flare out whenever he did so. Being behind the camera, I had to admit that capturing the dramatic nature of the ceremony was exhilarating. When I tilted up through the smoky air, rays of light shone through all the holes in his roof and cabin walls. I had the simultaneous feeling of awe for the beauty of the setting and of dismay that there were so many holes in his home. Tilting back down, I caught the dongba just as he was putting some blessing flour along the top of Cora's right hand. He bowed to her and then reached for my hand and did the same for me.

The last thing the dongba wanted to show us was his power of prophecy by offering to do a divination for me. Along with some of the dongba's male relatives who had now joined us to see what all the fuss was about, Ben was there to translate from Naxi to Mandarin, and Cora translated from Mandarin to English for me. Using some of the five elements—fire, wood, metal, water, and earth—the dongba could divine information concerning matters of romance, work, and family.

The dongba tossed some small white shells from a bag into a basket, touched them, and counted on his fingertips with his thumb and began, "Other people gave you many names throughout your life." One has to confirm or deny the statements made by the dongba during the divination. I confirmed this was true, as I had had a Vietnamese birth name, a French baptismal name, the last name of my first stepfather, and the last name of my first husband. He picked up the shells, blew into them, and tossed them again, saying, "They say you know things that normal people don't and generally you do a lot of work that other people don't know how to do." I hesitantly agreed, considering that I'd been told repeatedly through-out my journey that I had this gift, but was still getting used to the idea. "You have a big scar on your leg or arm," he continued. I confirmed that I had a long scar on my left leg due to an old knee surgery. The dongba touched the shells again, said something, and then all of a sudden Cora broke out in a fit of laughter and covered her mouth. I asked her what the dongba had said. Barely in control of her massive mirth she said, "He says you have two tigers—two boyfriends." Now, I had to think about that one. I was about to go into an explanation—*They weren't technically boyfriends, more like paramours, and one of them didn't live in town*—when Cora interrupted, saying, "He insists that you confirm or deny this." All I could do was shrug and say, "Uh … okay, yes … uh yuy yuy yuy," and the entire room filled with laughter. Moving from past to present, and now to the future, the dongba fiddled with some metal objects hanging on a ring and said in regard to our project, "Because the work will be difficult in the beginning, you shouldn't give up. You should keep going because I guarantee it's going to be a success." Cora added that the dongba kept repeating and insisting that it would be a success. I would come to rely heavily on this affirmation to keep me going in the face of doubt, struggle, and strife in the years it would take me to complete the film.

Like my great-grandfather, the dongba was a blind man with the gift of sight. Before our departure, he took out some paper that was white on one side and red on the other with prayers inscribed on it. He folded the paper, red prayer side in, and made a triangular talisman for each of us to carry over our hearts so that we might journey home safely. The only thing he'd asked in return for sharing his rituals and giving me a divination was to have a photo taken with Cora, Trinh, and me, even though he'd never see it. We all stood side-by-side, the dongba wrapping my hand in his, and Ben shot the photo. I felt sad to leave the dongba behind a locked gate, but I was honored to take his offering out into the world beyond the walls of the cultural center. As we headed home, I realized that every healer we had met had given me a gift of healing and a transmission of knowledge, and entrusted me to share their stories with others.

CHAPTER 12

The Retreat

Catskills, New York (Final Test — Another Death, Rebirth, and Resurrection)

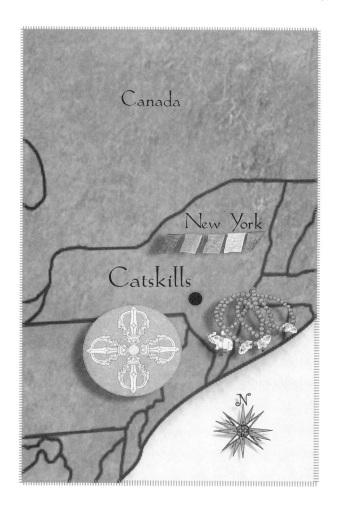

I arrived in Seattle just in time for the holidays and found myself hiding in my lakeside condo. There was a comfort in coming home and finding everything as I'd left it—convertible in the garage, four-poster bed made up, chair pushed under the desk—but also an emptiness. I couldn't connect to the holiday shoppers buzzing around trying to buy cheer, to the tired Christmas carols, nor to the multiple emails and phone messages. I was invited to holiday parties, to the movies and shows (all the things I usually enjoyed) by well-meaning friends, but I would decline, using the excuse that I needed to log and review all the footage so I could prepare for the editing process. The only thing that seemed to soothe me was looking out over the lake and looking back at the footage we'd shot. The contents of my life seemed the same, yet the context had profoundly shifted.

I stayed home, unable to sleep at night, getting up to watch the footage, taking nap breaks, and staying in my pajamas all day. Everyone else on the team had other projects to move on to, but I only cared about this one. Nothing mattered to me but to finish my film. It seemed I needed to know that the experiences I'd had were real and would not go missing in the muddle of my mind. I also felt now more than ever that these healing and spiritual traditions were endangered, and I felt even more compelled to shed light on this issue.

My best friend, Giselle, was concerned that I would starve to death, so she'd force me to go grocery shopping with her every Friday. Dubbing our outings "Fun Friday," she would also manage to slide in grabbing a coffee or browsing in a store for something she said she needed. I later realized this was her way of being able to see me physically and to know that I was bathing, eating, and hadn't gone off the deep end. Although I would humor her, I think we both knew I was already treading water in the deep end. My friend and the person who was the stay-at-home coordinator for

our shoot, Aine (pronounced "AHN-ya"), also understood that I was struggling with reentry to everyday reality. For many months, she was another
lifeline to the outside world, because she was helping me to organize the
footage and helping Cora to tie up loose ends from the shoot, so we would
talk on the phone almost daily.

One day, Aine casually said, "What about seeing that teacher in New
York?" I didn't know what she was talking about until she connected it to
the footage. "Remember in Ladakh? Didn't one of the amchis suggest you
see a teacher in New York? Maybe that would help you to feel better." She
said it as if it were the most obvious thing in the world. In that moment,
she pierced a fog I'd been in and let the sun peek through, though at first
it felt too bright. I replied, "Oh, that. Well, I don't know. What would
I say if I called him?" Aine was hyperintelligent and I always recognized
her tone when she had to talk to people who were light years behind her
in her thinking. Talking to me extra slowly but patiently, she continued,
"Well … you … could tell him … that the amchi sent you."

Monks in Quicksilver board shorts were doing cannonballs and belly flops
into a pool of pond water. Well, chlorine had been added and the filters
had been turned on, but the lake water they'd filled the Center's pool with
was still green and scummy looking. Aside from the questionable water,
I felt a little self-conscious being in a bathing suit in front of a rinpoche,
lamas, and strangers, but then one of the other women jumped in, so I
got the courage to do it, too. The water actually felt refreshing, and it gave
welcome relief from the hot, stagnant, and humid air. It also helped me to
wash away a thin layer of some of my egoic buildup that had been plaguing
me since my arrival at the Center. I'm sure there was some profound lesson
in Rinpoche's encouragement for all of us to jump in. The best part was
looking around at the group—the students, the teachers, the masters—to
see that we were all in the murky water together. We were at Tibetan Buddhist Summer Camp.

Now, if by any chance this sounds like a bunch of fun to you, think
again. Imagine being afforded the opportunity to face your ego and its

many trips not only every day, but also every moment of the day. The incessant jabber, obsessive thought, and pointless dross that populates those moments was astounding when I actually stopped and took notice. And I had time to take notice because while everyone else at the Center was participating in a two-week course on Rinpoche's teachings, I was left to wonder what I was doing there.

Four months prior, I had at last gotten up the nerve to do what Aine had advised, after languishing in a netherworld of in-between through the wet and dark Seattle winter. I'd had it in my head that I could do nothing else until I finished the film, so I had put off anything that didn't seem essential to keeping me alive or to getting me closer to a final cut. I'm not sure what I expected when I dug out Amchi Paljor's card and dialed the number on the back of it. Perhaps a cheerful Tibetan version of Mr. Miyagi from the film *The Karate Kid* saying, *"Tashi delek* ["hello" in Tibetan]. Yes, I teach you wax on, wax off. You come to New York, okay?" Instead, a very professional-sounding American woman answered the phone, "Hello? Blah blah blah Center, may I help you?" which completely threw me. *Yes, I needed help.*

When I finally found my words, I said hesitantly, "Uh … I'm looking for Rinpoche So-and-so. I was referred to him by Amchi Paljor in Ladakh."

"Uh-huh," she replied and waited for me to continue.

"Well, I guess he referred me because I had these weird episodes in Nepal and Ladakh and he thought Rinpoche could help me and that I really need some teaching because being an untrained oracle channel was dangerous for me and that I had to go to New York and study with Rinpoche and that I should call this number but I'm not sure really what I'm looking for and I'm working on this film about healing so maybe I could send him a copy of some of the footage," I rattled off hoping it made some semblance of sense to her.

"Okay, I'll leave him a message. May I have your number?" she replied cheerfully, as if what I'd said was completely commonplace.

Well, Rinpoche never called. But, because I'm a woman who never takes no, or a lack of response, which feels like a no, for an answer, I persisted, leaving messages every few days on the Center's system or with Theresa

(I learned her name since we were on more intimate terms now because I called so often). Being the compassionate Buddhist that she is, Theresa never made me feel insane or pesky. One day she suggested that I send Rinpoche a fax. She said, "Sometimes he gets some information from seeing your handwriting, so it may tell him something that your messages don't." I sent the fax and wrote in my best cursive all the things I had told Theresa over our several interactions.

Three days later, I got an email from the man himself. He wrote a terse message. "You may need a Tsa Lung master, teachings on opening and closing the Central Channel, and Dorje Sempa practice. Come to New York in July. Amchi Paljor will be there at that time." I had no idea what the rinpoche was talking about, but I was thrilled to get a personal email and to be invited to see him. And the fact that Amchi Paljor would be there at the same time felt both serendipitous and predestined. The thought of seeing him again and meeting the teacher he'd sent me to made me feel reassured that what I'd experienced on my extraordinary journey could be bridged with my ordinary life at home. That the big loose end I'd been dangling from could be tied.

I took a red-eye flight from Sea-Tac to JFK, a cab to Penn Station, a two-hour train ride to upstate New York, and a cab ride to the Center, which took twelve hours door-to-door. Riding the train was a great way to exhale, as out the windows the hustle and bustle of the city dissolved into the beauty of a wooded landscape and rolling river. I contemplated my horoscope, which I'd cut out from Rob Brezsny's "Free Will Astrology" column and pasted into my journal: "Yes, Capricorn, you're about to enjoy a phase in your astrological cycle when you'll receive lots of cosmic assistance if you commit yourself to a challenging process you're sure you can love over the long haul."

I arrived at the Center's retreat facilities, a former summer camp for families and kids, and followed the signs to the front office. Along with other arriving attendees getting registered, I gave my name, got a nametag, and was assigned a room. When I asked the welcoming women what my schedule would be, they looked at their list and saw that I was there independent of the group and one of them said, "We don't know. You'll have to see what Rinpoche says. But, you're welcome to join us for dinner and evening *tsok* (ritual gathering). Here's a key to your room. You're in the Buddha Building."

The Buddha Building was a long white one-story cinder-block structure with a tin roof that housed a stretch of several rooms leading to the community kitchen and bathrooms at one end. I walked by a few of the rooms before getting to mine, and when I entered I saw that it had a rustic cabin feel to it and was on the dark side, as it only had the light of one small window. To let a little more light in, most people chose to keep their doors open, with the screen door closed to keep the bugs out. Unlike the other retreat participants who had to double up, I was relieved to discover that I had my own room.

On my way to the bathroom, I was so excited to spot Amchi Paljor crossing the grass from another building. I ran up to him and said, "I'm here! You're here!" and was so relieved when he smiled and acknowledged me. Amchi Paljor looked around for a translator and found Lama Tenzin, a Tibetan monk who spoke Ladakhi, Tibetan, French, and English. I asked Amchi Paljor what I was supposed to do here and told him what Rinpoche had written in his email to me. Amchi Paljor said, "I don't know what you should do. We have to wait to see what Rinpoche says." Seeing how disappointed I was he added, "I'll try to speak with him about you and get a private audience with him for you." That helped to quell my anxiety for a little while.

There was just enough time to nap and shower before dinner, so I took the opportunity to do those things, arriving at dinner feeling fresh and spry. The others, who seemed to know each other well, had already gathered, so I spotted only one open table. Feeling like the awkward new kid in school, I braved sitting all by myself. All of a sudden all eyes were on me, and a few of the practitioners rushed over to me with urgency. "That's Rinpoche's table," one of them said. Saving me from my faux pas, they moved me to a free seat at one of their tables just before Rinpoche's arrival. Everyone stood up and we all put our hands together before our hearts and bowed when he and his entourage of lamas came in.

Rinpoche was nothing like I'd pictured him. He was youthful, a bit rotund, and was joking and laughing loudly with everyone before he sat down. Amchi Paljor was with him and was seated at the special table. I must have been staring at that table all during dinner, intent on meeting Rinpoche and asking him what I was supposed to be doing. The others noticed and tried to engage me in conversation. When one of them asked me why I was there, I was hard-pressed to find an answer, so I said, "I'm here for some teachings, but I'm not sure exactly what I'm supposed to learn. Rinpoche summoned me." That sounded really important and was an attempt to cover up the fact that the man didn't even know who I was or that I was there. But I didn't fool anyone, and one of the women sitting at my table, sensing my uneasiness, assured me, "Don't worry. Rinpoche is adept at seeing spirits, traveling out of body, and teaching about the mystical aspects of Tibetan Buddhism," Okay, so at least I felt I was in the right school.

We went from dinner straight in to the temple room for the tsok. Everyone was seated on the floor on cushions behind low red table benches upon which they had their mantra books. It was very much as the amchis and lamas had done in Ladakh. Once again, one of the students had compassion with my lost-puppy look and indicated a cushion next to her. I sat listening to Rinpoche speak and leading all of us into mantra recitation. It was really beautiful to be once again immersed in sacred ceremony, and for a while, I could forget about my questioning mind. That didn't last long, however. After tsok, I made a beeline for Rinpoche, and when I had my chance, I said, "Tashi delek, Rinpoche. I'm Marie-Rose." He shook my hand and said, "Tashi delek," and walked away to turn in for the night.

Cry, question, have nightmares, wake up, and repeat. I couldn't sleep at night as my mind was filled with negativity and melancholy. So I'd nap during the day while everyone else was in class. And while I was awake, I was plagued with the same questions: *Why am I here? Why would he call*

me here and just ignore me? I came all the way here and nothing is happening. I'm running out of time! Then the deeper questions would arise: *What if it wasn't an oracle, but just a nasty ghost that possessed me? What if all of it was just altitude sickness? What if I'm just a silly woman who thought she was on some big important mission, but it was just an ego trip?* And the worst one: *What if I don't have the gift of the oracle and am just plain batty?*

I was on one of those amazing jags when Lama Tenzin and Amchi Paljor knocked on my screen door. Embarrassed from them catching me in the middle of a full-throttle pity party, I tried to appear cheerful, but I would soon find out that they were very aware of what was happening with me. They let me know that Amchi Paljor had spoken with Rinpoche about my channeling and the deity's message. He hoped to arrange a meeting between Rinpoche and me for lunchtime. Oh, happy moment!

Lunchtime came and went and Rinpoche never even looked at me. Oh, unhappy moment. I almost felt as sorry for Amchi Paljor as I did for myself. The poor man was trying his best to help me, as I suspect he felt responsible for my being there. As a consolation prize, he agreed to give me a Tibetan Medicine 101 teaching. Well, I didn't have paper, pen, or my camera with me, so I listened to a bunch of stuff that was way over my head. Because the lovely translator, Lama Tenzin, was currently visiting from his home in Paris, sometimes he'd translate the teachings in English and sometimes in French. I really appreciated their efforts to help fill my time while Rinpoche was ignoring me.

Seeing how hard Lama Tenzin and Amchi Paljor were trying to help me feel better made me realize I was acting like a spoiled child. I had to take a hard look at myself by stopping to think about myself. When I did, I took note that Amchi Paljor did not look well. In fact, he'd seemed wan and tired since I first laid eyes on him at the Center. He was much thinner and frailer than I'd remembered him being in Ladakh. At one point during our lesson, Amchi Paljor said he was too tired to continue. I asked him how long he had not been feeling well and he said he'd had a fever for two weeks. I told him I found that alarming. Feeling obligated to help Rinpoche with the teachings, Amchi Paljor had traveled all the way from Ladakh, and pushed on since his arrival, and now it was all catching up to him. Being the only amchi present, there were no doctors to treat him. He asked if I could help him.

I was surprised and honored by his request. He was familiar with my channeling experiences, but how could he know that when I had studied with my teacher in Seattle before her betrayal, I had become pretty good at the laying-on-of-hands healing that she'd taught me? Although my mind tried to tell me I wasn't trained enough to help heal a senior amchi, my heart knew I could not refuse him. I told him I could try and he said he was in such need of healing that he would appreciate whatever I could do for him. As I felt the old familiar feeling of energy moving down my head, through my heart and out my hands, Amchi Paljor fell asleep. All my self-indulgent thinking melted away as his fever lifted. When he awoke, he said he felt better, as did I. Afterward, I went back to my room to relax and regroup. I know something significant had happened, and yet helping him felt like the most natural and easy thing for me to do.

After that experience, I decided that if I got nothing more than to spend this quality time with Amchi Paljor (and Lama Tenzin), then that would be plenty. I started interacting more with the other students between their classes and asking about them rather than being so focused on me. I explored the grounds and started to take in the peace and beauty that surrounded me. When I couldn't sleep at night, I delighted in watching the fireflies dancing outside my room. Letting go of what I came to get, I began to ask if there was anything I could do to help with the classes or to support the teachers, as I had more free time than they did. I accepted that if Rinpoche couldn't see me on this trip, then it just wasn't the right time. This set me free from most of my melancholy and self-obsessive thoughts.

"Do you have man troubles or male influences?" Rinpoche asked in a matter-of-fact way, as he scanned above and around me, not looking into my eyes. "Well, I've had some," I replied hesitantly. "Um hum," he said, and typed in his computer. He continued the interview, "and does it make you feel regretful or badly?" "Sure, I'd say it does to a certain extent," I answered while thinking, *What does this have to do with channeling?* "Um hum," he said again, and typed some more. Then he began to speak rapid-fire: "Thus far, I am waiting for a vision or a dream to know if I am to do anything for you or to work with you directly. My first assessment is that your channel picks up helpful as well as disruptive energies, and if it is overexposed, this can lead to false predictions. It's difficult for me to assess the particular deity unless I can see you actually channeling, because what may at first appear to be positive could gradually show its true colors as disruptive."

My long-awaited meeting with Rinpoche lasted all of five minutes. He'd finally summoned me, sending one of the assistant lamas to my room. I wasn't sure why, but suspected it was because I'd finally let go of needing him to see me. Rinpoche went on to explain that my life force would get weakened if my channel picked up disruptive entities, and that these beings could live off of my essential fluid and contaminate the brilliant light of my mind. Then he said something in Tibetan to an assistant, who then brought in Lama Tenzin. Rinpoche spoke to Lama Tenzin in Tibetan, then turned to me and said, "Go with him and he'll give you what you need for now."

Once again I had the opportunity to watch how my mind would label things happy-making or unhappy-making. He had summoned me after I'd let go of expectation. Oh, happy moment. He was still waiting for a sign to decide if he should do anything for me. Oh, unhappy moment. I did have a gift. Oh, happy moment. But, he didn't know if the entity it picked up was an enlightened deity or an energetic vampire. Oh, unhappy moment. He hadn't looked at the videos I'd left for him of me channeling. Oh, another unhappy moment. I'd get to work with Lama Tenzin. Oh, happy moment. I had an audience with Rinpoche, but he didn't let me ask any questions. Oh, happy-unhappy moment. I could see so clearly for the first time how crazy-making all this labeling and thinking was. That's when I realized that more important than learning about channeling, oracles, deities, or demons was my need to learn to tame the demons of my mind's own making.

Lama Tenzin and I worked together daily for the remainder of my stay at the Center. The first thing he acknowledged is that when our vessel is not purified we can have disturbances that cause nightmares, fitful sleep, melancholy, and anxiety. This is why he and Amchi Paljor had such compassion for me and understood what I had been going through since my arrival. He also said that as I began to absorb the teachings and to do the practices, the disturbances might continue as the purification burns them off, but that these negative channels would eventually subside. Lama Tenzin was authorized to give me transmissions, teachings, and mantras. I'd asked if I could take notes, but he said traditionally the student is supposed to just listen. Wax on, wax off was on!

Rinpoche had also enlisted one of the advanced students, a gorgeous French woman with dark hair and blue eyes, to teach me some yoga movements to help me clear my channel and strengthen it. When she did the movements, they seemed so graceful and effortless. I was uncoordinated at first, and then after a few sessions began to feel confident that I was getting them down. Years later, I would watch a video of a Tibetan master doing this practice, and when he did it, not only did it appear as if he were in fast motion, but he actually lifted himself off the ground. That's when I realized the French beauty had given me the *Yoga For Dummies* version of the practice. She'd also instructed me per Rinpoche's orders not to talk about my practice or the results of it with anyone, for it could dilute their effectiveness.

A lot was crammed into those few days of teachings and training, and it would take me years to process and understand what I was actually given. The most important takeaway that I am still cognizant of on a daily basis is that the gurus, teachings, and practices are not the thing. They merely point us in the direction of, or help us get to, the thing. Whether we have the gift of the oracle, the talent of music, or the work of a laborer, we have the same ultimate job: committing to eliminate the obscurations to knowing our pure nature. The single-pointed commitment is the driving force that keeps us on track and brings us back, even when we may stray. Unlike the mea culpa I was raised with, these lessons taught me that looking at our faults and bad habits is necessary, not so we can beat ourselves up about them, but so that the dirt can be exposed and cleared. My nightmares, anxieties, and self-abusive habits did lift a bit while I was at the Center, but when they would return I was reminded to simply let them pass to be purified. And even now when the everyday concerns of worldly matters take hold of my mind and fill me with fear or despair, I can remember my commitment and I become more impervious to their destructive natures.

I was blessed with one more audience with Rinpoche before my departure, this one for a brief two minutes. By now I understood Rinpoche did not need to spend a bunch of one-on-one time with me to know what I needed. Once again he scanned above and around me, but this time he did look me in the eye briefly. Rinpoche explained that it was determined that indeed there were many energies—dark and light—that were attracted to my light channel, and therefore I needed protection. Placing in my palm a square blue and gold brocade cloth pouch, he said, "This is infused with protective mantras handed down from my lineage. You must keep it on you at all times, even while bathing." And, I was shown out of his office. Both meetings showed me that all along, Rinpoche had been meditating about my situation, was mindful of prescribing the precise spiritual protocol for me, and that his appearance of having ignored me was helping me to burn off my ego's need for self-importance and validation.

When the day came for me to leave, I understood that I did not come here to learn to be a channel for an oracle. That was a choice to be made at a later time. Instead, it was for me to have confirmation that I did have a gift and that it needed to be guarded until I was spiritually mature enough to decide what to do with it. As I loaded my bags into the cab, I felt grateful, for I had received so much more than I could ever have imagined. To my surprise and delight, Amchi Paljor came to see me off. Lama Tenzin was busy helping with the group teachings and was unavailable, so while Amchi Paljor was waiting for another translator, he removed the mala beads from around his neck and placed them around mine. The string of sandalwood beads, which he had rolled between his fingers for years, were infused with all the mantras he had recited while they had been his. Amchi Paljor also handed me an envelope that contained four small red and gold cloth pouches tied with red thread and instructions. The instructions, written in English, said each pouch contained a *rilbu* (precious pill), the most powerful of Tibetan medicine remedies, and that they were to be taken whenever I needed to clean spiritual contamination and increase my life-force energy. To date, I've taken three of them.

When our pinch-hitter translator finally emerged from the building, he looked rather familiar. Newang, who was strikingly handsome, introduced himself and said, "You may have met my brother in Nyee. He was a lama-in-training there." Then it dawned on me; this was Hollywood's brother! As Amchi Paljor was speaking excitedly, Newang looked confused and then said to me, "He's saying something about 'the deity's message has been heard.' Does that make sense to you?" I grinned and said, "Indeed it does." Then, as the cab drive honked his horn, Newang added, "He says, 'Don't worry. In the future, it will be done.'" As I drove off in the cab, Amchi Paljor stood there waving and watching me go. I wept, holding on to his mala beads and inhaling deeply their sweet scent of sandalwood.

CHAPTER 13

Pule (Prayer)

Return to Hawaii (Return with the Elixir)

My time at the Center seemed to encapsulate all the lessons from my journey and cull them down to a single point. Commit everything I do, say, or think toward removing obscurations so that I may eventually see clearly through enlightened eyes, not so I can look in the mirror and be impressed or depressed by what I see. Within the blanket of that commitment, all the grasping that fear and hope tend to create can be transmuted to love and compassion. My obsessions with whether I had a gift or was insane, whether it was dangerous or safe, whether my film would get made or not, whether I could save the endangered traditions or have to watch them disappear, were all based in fear that I would fail, but also in hope that my work could make a positive impact on the world. If I failed, I would perceive myself to be a bad person. If I succeeded, I could see myself as a good person. I learned over the course of these teachings that fear and hope were two sides of the same limiting coin.

Fear and hope were all about being self-focused, whereas love and compassion are about zooming out and seeing the landscape in the context of all sentient beings. And yet, even offering up my frailties and faults into the coffer of commitment could allow them to mature into love and compassion. The trick is not about trying to get there—that ideal spiritual perfection—but to understand that it's the continued practice here in the muck of our human existence that is perfect. With all that said, there is still a meandering winding road that lies between receiving the lesson and mastering the truth of the teaching.

That summer of my Tibetan Buddhist camp, I was also called to return to Hawaii. Nancy Kahalewai, our first project sponsor, had let me know that two of our healers, Aunty Mary and Papa K, were in dire straits. Aunty

Mary had injured her ankle and was unable to get to her healing room. More than the pain of her injury, it was her inability to help others that caused her the greatest suffering. Papa K was in the hospital due to complications of his diabetes. I made arrangements and caught a plane to the Big Island, this time without my fellow LBC members. It had been over a year since I'd been to Hawaii, and I felt compelled to see our beloved, wounded healers, if only to offer them some cheer and comfort.

Landing at the open-air airport, setting foot on the aina, and feeling the breeze caressing my face, I felt I was home again. Then and for many years following, each time I left the island I would sob inexplicably, and each time I landed I would be filled with the joyful sense of homecoming. Once again, Nancy opened up her house to me. She had spruced up the place and it felt roomier and lighter, so for me it was like returning to the comfort of the familiar, but with a new twist. As she did on our last visit, Nancy organized outings, meetings, and some fun. Although our first priority was for me to see Aunty Mary and Papa K, it took a few days for us to get through to them. I was able to share with Nancy some of the amazing adventures I'd had since we were last together, and some of the *pilikia* (trouble, worries), mostly financial, that still plagued me after my teacher's shenanigans and the challenges of seeking additional funding to finish the film. She knew just the thing I needed to help me maintain a pono state of mind.

Nancy arranged for us to participate in a sunset meditation near the top of Mauna Kea with a Hawaiian elder who had the privilege of leading such groups on the 13,800-foot-tall dormant volcano, considered sacred by Hawaiians. As it turned out, we'd missed the group at the meeting place. Since my economy rental car could not make the climb all the way up the dirt road to the meditation site, we hiked. Just as in Nepal and Ladakh, the altitude was a challenge. I found myself putting one foot in front of the other and getting in the rhythm of exhale, exhale, inhale. When we arrived, I was crestfallen to find that the ceremony was over. The group members were in the middle of sharing about their experiences, yet they invited us into their circle and asked us to tell them what we had wished for in coming. Nancy said she had wanted to ask the mountain to bring her closer to Spirit. I had planned to ask for an *oki* (cutting) ceremony, to disengage from anything that was keeping me from the present and from moving forward. After I said it, I was surprised to find I was crying, like the kid who'd saved up her money and arrived to find the circus had left. The elder who'd led the group put his hand on my shoulder and told me not to worry. He added, "In walking up here, you walked your talk and it has been done. Let it be so." In essence, our commitment to get to the mountain despite our car trouble was the offering, and so the blessing had already been given.

After three months of being away, Aunty Mary made it back to her healing room. She'd wrapped her arms around my neck, and together we hobbled from her house, across the carport, and into the former storage space that over the years had become her healing room. This time she was there to receive healing, not give it. Aunty Mary had lamented that she'd been in such pain and it hurt her heart not to be able to do her work, yet for one reason or another, all the students she'd taught lomilomi to were off-island or unavailable to help her. Seeing her so miserable, I asked if there was anything I could do to help her.

"I need help to get back to work," she replied.

"I don't know how to do lomilomi, and I'm not a healer like you, but sometimes when I put my hands on people, it makes them feel better. Would you like me to try to do something for you?" She smiled, eagerly agreed, and braved getting up from the house and moving to the healing room.

Since I'd been told so often on my journey that I had a gift, whether I could channel an oracle or not, I prayed and offered whatever gift I might have to be of greatest assistance to Aunty Mary. She lay on the floor, where she'd put me just over a year ago, and closed her eyes. Once again, I had the feeling of fullness in my heart and the sense of warmth in my hands. I worked on her entire body and then focused on her hurt foot and ankle. Going in and out of sleep, Aunty would wake up and say, "Oh, that feels good," or make sounds as if she were eating something delicious. She made a wish that she could walk again like she used to before the polio ravaged her body at age six. I could sense that in the healing room she felt powerful having triumphed over the disabilities that came with the illness. But, having been kept from her work for so long, the grief of the limitations it caused had come back to haunt her.

When we finished the healing, she whispered, "You have nice healing hands." Then she sat up, crawled to a cabinet, opened a canister, and said, "I want to give you something," and then put money in my hand. I tried to refuse it several times, but she said it was what she wanted. Not wanting to upset her, I finally agreed to accept it, but said that I would put it toward the project, to which she replied, "Or toward a snack, or whatever," and giggled. I gave her a big hug, and when she thanked me, I said, "Don't mention!" mimicking her way of saying, "You're welcome." I felt so grateful and fulfilled that I was actually able to relieve some of her pain, and that I could give back to Aunty Mary in light of all she'd given to me and to others.

"Oh, it's good. It has a little tickle to it," Papa K said, smiling as he held the ukulele up to his ear and plucked a few strings. I had remembered that Papa K was a musician who used to perform in Las Vegas, and thought it might cheer him up to be able to play and sing while he was stuck in the hospital. I'd told the young man at the music shop that I was going to visit a sick kahuna and was looking for something to bring to him. I couldn't really afford one of the really nice ukuleles, but I was going to put the money Aunty Mary had given me toward the gift. The shopkeeper took one off the wall and said, "It's not the best, but it should be good enough to get him goin'. You just take it," and refused to accept any money for it. I felt moved to experience once again the aloha spirit.

When I got to Papa K's room, I was surprised to find that he was alone. Having taught so many students on the island and being so well loved by his community, I thought for sure I'd have to wade through a crowd just to say "Aloha." He smiled a wide, toothless grin at seeing me and we gave each other a big hug. Papa K was surprised, too, that I was alone without my crew, but I told him they were all working on other things. As happy as we were to be reunited, it was painful for me to see him in a hospital gown, confined to the hospital bed. In addition to bringing the ukulele, I had also brought my camera. I'd guessed that playing, singing, and talking story on camera might allow him to forget for a while that he was a patient and feel more like a star. He loved the idea, and I put my camera on a shelf next to his bed, zoomed out to a wide shot, and hit *record.*

After we caught up and exchanged stories of our adventures since we'd last been together, the conversation took a serious turn. "I don't want to lose my leg," Papa K said somberly, "because it's important to me." Until then, I hadn't realized the gravity of the situation. Within a day, the doctors would decide whether or not to amputate his right leg from the knee down. I asked why his many students weren't here to help him. He'd shared that they were scared and weren't ready. He added, "I have to find someone just as good as me to do this. You know, to help heal me. Because a healer cannot heal his own self, especially one like me."

"But certainly your students could use something of what you've taught them to help you," I replied.

"What I need isn't lomilomi," he said. "What I need is the breath of *ha.*" He explained that the practice of ha (breath) was one of the most powerful of the ancient Hawaiian healing practices, in which a kahuna would say special prayers and then use his breath to heal anything from broken bones to terminal illnesses. And that was something he had yet to teach anyone.

Finding a kahuna well versed in the practice of ha was not as easy as finding a ukulele in Hawaii. I wracked my brain trying to figure out how we could make this happen before the doctors made a decision that would be irrevocable once executed. Papa K must have read my mind because he said, "We just don't have enough time." At that point, an idea came to me. Even if my light channel wasn't ready to carry an oracle, could it possibly run Papa K's healing abilities, so that they could flow back to him through me? Could he infuse my breath with the power of healing ha energy? I looked at him and said casually, "Well, since I'm the only one here, you wanna teach me?" He smiled and said, "Yeah. If you want to learn, I'll teach." Again, I felt he must have read my mind because both of us knew full well that you don't just give a five-minute lesson on the practice of ha.

I moved over to the right side of his hospital bed and sat next to Papa K. I prayed that I could be of greatest service to him and that I be a clear vessel through which the healing he needed could come through. Papa K said, "You just repeat after me," and he began a Hawaiian prayer. When I stumbled over the words, he'd repeat them until I got it right. After we closed with "Amen," he said, "You do it three times, like this, right over the knee." He then took my arm and exhaled powerfully into it three times, making the "ha" sound. Then, using the side of his hand, he gently slid it over my wrist and hand after each breath, as if to scoop away the illness. "When you are ready you can do it," he said.

Then I felt light-headed and my hands began to move over his knee and down to his foot. Like Aunty Mary, Papa K went in and out of sleep. As the energy ran through my hands, they shook, and at times I could feel pain and disease coming out of his body and would flick them away into the air. With my eyes half closed I could feel the light changing in the room, and my back would be warmed by the sun shining through the windows or cooled as clouds passed through. At one point, Papa K stirred and said, "I don't know if anyone's ever told you this, but you've got real good hands for healing." I closed the session by exhaling powerfully three times, making the sound "ha!" over his knee and sweeping away illness with my left hand after each breath. I sat back in my chair and watched Papa K resting with a peaceful expression on his face. When he opened his eyes, he smiled and said, almost surprised, "It does feel better. Yeah, you got the touch for it." A few days later, Papa K was able to leave the hospital with no need for amputation.

All this time, I had been in denial or in fear of what having a gift to see beyond this realm or to heal others could mean. After witnessing so many rituals, ceremonies, and healings by others who had committed to this work, I was plagued with doubts that I could handle the responsibility that came with it, or that its effects through me could even be real. Perhaps seeing the misuse of it by my former teacher had caused me to reject it within myself. But being empowered to help Amchi Paljor, Aunty

Mary, and Papa K allowed me to settle the questions that had troubled me throughout my journey: "Do I have a gift?" and "If so, what do I do with it?" It was simple. If indeed I had a gift, whether it be for channeling, healing, or filmmaking, and I could commit its use toward service to others and my own evolution, then let it be so. I started to believe that being a healer didn't have to become my identity, but rather could simply be one of the precious jewels among the riches of my life that I could offer to share with others when appropriate.

Before I left Papa K, he picked up the ukulele, started strumming, and said, "This I dedicate to you. This I wrote." He cleared his throat and began to play and sing. Despite his weakened state, he serenaded sweetly and then belted out the last note, shredding the closing chords on his ukulele like a true showman.

> *Leimana*
> *There is heaven in your eyes*
> *You make a dreary day*
> *Seem bright and gay*
> *Leimana*
>
> *For the red of the roses*
> *Are in your cheeks*
> *The blue of the skies*
> *In your eyes*
> *The sweetness of honey*
> *Is in your voice*
> *I'm glad the gods*
> *Have made the choice*
>
> *Leimana*
> *You will always be the same*
> *There are angels, it's true*
> *But none like you, my*
> *Leimana*

There are angels, it's true
But none like you
My ... Lei ... ma ... na-a-a-a

EPILOGUE

Shifting Sands
Tulum, Mexico
(Imbibing and Sharing the Elixir)

It ended up taking me eleven years to complete the film. Now, as I sit in my cabana on the Mayan Riviera staring at the ever-changing Caribbean Sea and laying down the final words of this book, it will have been seven years since I first started trying to put all my experiences into a cohesive written narrative. I used to believe it was lack of funding that caused the film and book to take so long to be completed, but in the end, I realized that it took me that long to be able to process enough of what was given to me to be able to share it with others on a greater level.

I came to Tulum, Mexico, to unplug and to drop in so I could focus on the completion of the book, but never content to do just one thing, I have also been exploring the various healing and spiritual traditions of the Mayan culture. While my belly and organs were being massaged into place with a Mayan *yoot keene* (abdominal massage) treatment, I wondered if this was how that giant frog may have felt each time the dongba beat his belly to get the prayers out of it. I've sweated out my fears and hopes during the *temazcal* ceremony, the equivalent of Native American sweat lodge but done in a brick or stone and stucco dome, to ring in the lunar new year and get to the homestretch of this story with renewed clarity. I've swum in *cenotes* (sacred grotto pools), walked among sacred pyramid ruins, and floated down ancient canals to receive blessings from the spirits of this land so that this book may bring some comfort, inspiration, or joy to its readers.

I never did hang a shingle that said "Healer" or "Oracle Medium," but somehow, through word of mouth, I was blessed with a successful healing practice in Taos, New Mexico, Seattle, and Los Angeles, and have brought people from all over the world on healing intensive retreats in Hawaii. Having worked with several committed individuals toward experiencing greater awareness, peace, and joy, I moved from doing the one-to-one work toward the one-to-many. I started a nonprofit organization, Healing Planet Project, whose mission it is to create media as medicine and to build awareness around healing and spiritual traditions worldwide through film, photography, books, and interactive media.

Having traveled and visited cultures under the siege of ethnocide, I intend for this book to reflect the story of our collective journey through loss of spiritual identity and the promise of its transformation into something that is pertinent in our collective world of modernity. The healers and spiritual leaders I have met along my journey did not ask me to preserve their traditions and practices, but rather to share them with those outside their culture, to translate their spiritual legacy in a way that may be relevant in another context. In the years since I started my journey, many of those I met have passed on, or, as the Hawaiians say, changed address. I've written *Talking Story* as a story of hope that the essence of our spiritual self survives and can flourish even after adversity, change, and apparent loss. No matter where I go, I am reminded daily of the teachings I have been blessed to have been given, and I'm grateful for the opportunities I've been afforded to practice what I've learned.

Every morning here, the gardeners clean the debris off the sand walking paths and then rake designs into them. I always have a twinge of regret being the first one to put footprints in their works of art. This morning, the artist and I crossed paths, he going in one direction with his rake and me going in the other destroying what he'd just done. We both said, "Hola! Buenos días," and continued on. At one point, I'd stopped to admire two radiating suns he'd just made. I looked back at him and he stood there watching me. I pointed to his suns, put my thumbs up, and smiled at him. Resting his elbow on his rake, his smile grew to a grin. I walked around his suns, not able to bring myself to traipse through them. As much as I've been taught about accepting the nature of impermanence, some things are worth holding on to, even if only for another brief moment.

Marie-Rose Phan-Lê
Tulum, Mexico
February 21, 2014

ACKNOWLEDGMENTS

The documentary film and this book are the fulfillment of a promise and the realization of a dream. Because those who contributed to the creation of the film were acknowledged in the film credits, here I will only address acknowledgments specific to the writing of this book.

I'd like to thank Nancy Nordhoff and the staff at Hedgebrook for granting me a six-week writer's residency in which nurturing, encouragement, and sacred sanctuary were provided so that I might plant the first seeds of the manuscript. I am deeply grateful to my creativity coach extraordinaire, Brooke Warner, who grabbed my hand and never let go throughout all the struggles and triumphs of birthing this book, which would never have been completed without her expertise, deft insights, and encouragement for me to lay my heart on the page.

I am honored that North Atlantic Books saw the potential of the book, continued to stay interested over the years, and then committed to partnering with me to publish and launch *Talking Story* into the world. Thank you Richard Grossinger, Doug Reil, Erin Wiegand, Emily Boyd, Janet Levin, Susan Bumps, Jessica Sevey, and Vanessa Ta.

I would like to express my love and gratitude to mom for starting me down this path of living the mundane while reaching for the heavens; my family and friends who supported and encouraged me to keep going; Bernard "Dadou" Mayer for his love and for cocreating our mandala home in paradise where I could write and share with others the healing transmissions I have been given; Cora E. Edmonds for being the first to dream this project with me and believe in all its possibilities; my beloved brother Thanh Lequang and his wife, Annie, for their generosity in sharing with me more details of Aunty Lien's life; Thomas L. Kelly, my dharma brother, who opened the gates to the world of the dhamis and amchis, kept me connected to that realm, and was there to answer my questions when my memory failed me; Jigme Lama for validating my recollections of village life, names, and facts of our time in Humla; George W. Perkins for being a tireless champion of this project, who was among the first readers of my initial chapters and continued to gently prod me to finish; and to Brice W. Karsh for lovingly poring over my chapters, asking the "everyman questions" to keep me accountable for taking care of my readers, and for making it possible for me to retreat in Tulum, Mexico, to finish the final chapters.

Finally, I am forever grateful to all the healers and teachers who left us with breadcrumbs to follow and signposts to point the way home.

Pablo Amaringo Shuña, "Don Pablo"—Peru (rest in peace)
Mary Fragas, "Aunty Mary"—Hawaii (rest in peace)
Sylvester K. Kepilino, "Papa K"—Hawaii (rest in peace)
Robert Po'okapu Keli'iho'omalu Sr., "Uncle Robert"—Hawaii
Mahealani Henry, "Aunty Mahealani"—Hawaii
Nancy Kahalewai—Hawaii
Tran Thi Lien, "Aunty Lien"—Vietnam (rest in peace)
Takka Bahadur Rokaya—Nepal (rest in peace)
Dragpa Choden "Agu Lama"—Nepal (rest in peace)
Dhami Mangale—Nepal (rest in peace)
Sonam Gyalpo—Nepal
Samten Chobal—Nepal
Tsering Chobal Lama—Nepal
Sher Bahadur—Nepal
Rigzin Namgyal, "Lama Rigzin"—Ladakh
Tsering Paljor, "Amchi Paljor"—Ladakh (rest in peace)
The Dongba—Lijiang
Lama Tenzin—New York
Rinpoche—New York

C. Ryan Brady

ABOUT THE AUTHOR

Marie-Rose Phan-Lê has more than twenty years' experience in film and television production (*Northern Exposure, Prefontaine, Ace's High*). She is the founder and president of Healing Planet Project, a nonprofit organization dedicated to the preservation and presentation of ancient healing and spiritual traditions. Marie-Rose traveled extensively from the beaches of Hawaii to the heights of the Himalayas, for her award-winning documentary film, *Talking Story*, the companion to this book. She has transitioned her flourishing healing practice working one-to-one with individuals to focusing on the one-to-many, consulting with organizations, businesses, and other groups. She is currently the chief operating officer and creative director at High Impact Inc. Phan-Lê was born in Vietnam, emigrated to France, and later to the United States, and currently lives in Hawaii.